Publishing during Doctoral Candidature

Jun Lei

Publishing during Doctoral Candidature

Policies, Practices, and Identities

Jun Lei
Faculty of Foreign Languages
Ningbo University
Ningbo, Zhejiang, China

ISBN 978-981-99-0990-2   ISBN 978-981-99-0988-9 (eBook)
https://doi.org/10.1007/978-981-99-0988-9

© The Editor(s) (if applicable) and The Author(s), under exclusive license to Springer Nature Singapore Pte Ltd. 2023
This work is subject to copyright. All rights are solely and exclusively licensed by the Publisher, whether the whole or part of the material is concerned, specifically the rights of translation, reprinting, reuse of illustrations, recitation, broadcasting, reproduction on microfilms or in any other physical way, and transmission or information storage and retrieval, electronic adaptation, computer software, or by similar or dissimilar methodology now known or hereafter developed.
The use of general descriptive names, registered names, trademarks, service marks, etc. in this publication does not imply, even in the absence of a specific statement, that such names are exempt from the relevant protective laws and regulations and therefore free for general use.
The publisher, the authors, and the editors are safe to assume that the advice and information in this book are believed to be true and accurate at the date of publication. Neither the publisher nor the authors or the editors give a warranty, expressed or implied, with respect to the material contained herein or for any errors or omissions that may have been made. The publisher remains neutral with regard to jurisdictional claims in published maps and institutional affiliations.

This Springer imprint is published by the registered company Springer Nature Singapore Pte Ltd.
The registered company address is: 152 Beach Road, #21-01/04 Gateway East, Singapore 189721, Singapore

To my wife, Jimei, and our sons, Zimo and Zirui

Preface

"Time is pressing!" That was the remark that I kept hearing while speaking with a group of doctoral students to recruit participants for a research project on doctoral publication. What they meant by that was the time pressure they encountered in their efforts to fulfill their university's publication requirements. As one participant aptly noted, "It's impossible to publish your own (thesis) research to meet the university's publication requirements." Then I started to wonder why it was so challenging to fulfill the university's publication requirements and how they managed to do it.

Thus began my five-year study of Chinese nursing doctoral students' scholarly publishing experiences and practices. Informed by the theoretical frameworks of neoliberalism and activity theory, the study examined six Chinese nursing doctoral students' scholarly publishing activities within the context of their doctoral studies. Drawing on the findings of the study, this book brings together policies, practices, identities, and their connections pertaining to doctoral publication. It demonstrates how policies, practices, and identities intersect with each other and reveals how policies can shape doctoral students' publishing practices and evolving identities. The intended readers for this book include postgraduates, researchers, and practitioners in the fields of applied linguistics and doctoral education. Doctoral students seeking to publish their work and supervisors looking to support their doctoral students' publishing efforts may also find it useful.

I would like to thank all the participants for sharing with me their thoughts, texts, sorrows, joys, setbacks, and triumphs throughout this study and beyond. Without their generosity and kindness, this book would not have been possible. The book has also benefited from feedback, inspiration, and assistance from many mentors, colleagues, and friends. I am grateful to Guangwei Hu, Sue Starfield, Yongyan Li, Yinling Cheung, Peter Teo, Ramona Tang, and Willy Renandya for their constructive feedback on earlier drafts of this book. My gratitude also goes to Lawrence Jun Zhang, Xiao Lan Curdt-Christiansen, Ruilin Li, Weihua Hu, Tan Jin, Guihua Wang,

Chaoqun Xie, Keyi Zhang, and many others who inspired, encouraged, and assisted me during the research and writing process. I am also greatly indebted to Ningbo University, China for providing me with a grant to prepare this book and to Nanyang Technological University, Singapore for offering me a scholarship to conduct the research.

Ningbo, China   Jun Lei

Contents

1 **Introduction** 1
   1.1 Publishing During Doctoral Candidature 2
   1.2 Overview of the Research 7
   1.3 Organisation of the Book 11
   References 12

2 **Doctoral Publication as a Sociopolitical Practice** 17
   2.1 Social Constructivist Perspectives on Doctoral Publication 17
   2.2 Neoliberal Perspectives on Doctoral Publication 24
   2.3 Activity Theory Perspectives on Doctoral Publication 26
   2.4 Conclusion 28
   References 28

3 **Doctoral Publication Policies: Neoliberal Ideologies and Stakeholder Perspectives** 37
   3.1 Institutional Policies on Doctoral Publication 37
   3.2 Supervisor and Student Perspectives 41
   3.3 (Dis)connections Between Institutional Policies and Stakeholder Perspectives 43
   3.4 Conclusion 47
   References 48

4 **Doctoral Publication Practices: Competing Demands and Coping Strategies** 51
   4.1 Boundary Crossing Through Starting Early 51
   4.2 Refashioning the Scholarly Publishing Activity System 56
   4.3 Managerial Roles of the University and Supervisor 61
   4.4 Transformed Practices and Truncated Experiences 66
   4.5 Conclusion 72
   References 73

5	**Doctoral Students' Dual Identities: Constraints and Affordances of Doctoral Publication**	79
	5.1 Challenges in Applying Conceptual Tools for Scholarly Publishing	79
	5.2 Mediating Resources for Coping with the Challenges	85
	5.3 Constraints and Affordances of Doctoral Publication	93
	5.4 Conclusion	96
	References	96
6	**Conclusion**	101
	6.1 Connections Between Policies, Practices, and Identities	101
	6.2 Situated Conceptualisation of Doctoral Publication	104
	6.3 Limitations and Future Research Directions	106
	6.4 Implications for Theory, Policy, and Pedagogy	108
	References	111

List of Figures

Fig. 3.1	Tensions concerning scholarly publishing within the doctoral study activity system	45
Fig. 4.1	New tensions generated by the adoption of the strategy of starting early	54
Fig. 4.2	New tensions generated by the adoption of the orchestrating strategy	58
Fig. 4.3	Roles-related tensions concerning scholarly publishing within the doctoral study activity system	62
Fig. 5.1	Tools-related tensions concerning scholarly publishing within the doctoral study activity system	80

List of Tables

Table 1.1	A summary of the data collection methods and the data collected	10
Table 3.1	A summary of the activity systems and thematic analyses of the doctoral students' challenges and contradictions in scholarly publishing	46
Table 4.1	Changes required for successful boundary crossing through starting early	55
Table 5.1	A summary of the doctoral students' difficulties in scholarly publishing	81
Table 5.2	A summary of the mediating resources for resolving the tensions in scholarly publishing	86

Chapter 1
Introduction

Doctoral education has undergone tremendous changes over the past few decades as a result of the intensifying globalisation and marketisation of higher education across the world (e.g., Becher & Trowler, 2001; Nerad, 2020; Ruano-Borbalan, 2022). One such change concerns the ever-increasing pressure on doctoral students to publish during their candidature. Research has shown that doctoral students are being increasingly expected or required to publish during their candidature, as evidenced in the mantra of "publish or no degree" (Casanave, 2010; Flowerdew & Habibie, 2022; Li, 2016; Nagano & Spiczéné, 2018). There is evidence showing that apart from meeting graduation requirements or expectations, doctoral students have other motives for scholarly publishing, such as learning the ropes of scholarly publishing (Bardi, 2015; Mizzi, 2014), securing post-doctoral jobs (Kwan, 2010, 2013; McGrail et al., 2006), laying foundations for a productive career in the future (Hartley & Betts, 2009; Kamler, 2008), winning scholarships or other types of award (Lillis & Curry, 2010; Paré, 2010), and producing knowledge (Aitchison et al., 2012; Raddon, 2011). These motives suggest that scholarly publishing during doctoral candidature is a high-stakes activity. Aside from being a high-stakes activity, it is also a highly challenging one (see, e.g., Casanave, 2010; Hartley & Betts, 2009). Research on doctoral students' attempts to publish during candidature, for example, has revealed two challenges inherent in doctoral education, namely, competing demands for students' limited time (Lee & Aitchison, 2011; Lundell & Beach, 2003) and doctoral students' fledgling scholarly abilities (Aitchison & Lee, 2006; Mizzi, 2014).

Despite the high stakes and challenges of doctoral publication, however, there is a relatively small body of research that has focused specifically on doctoral students' scholarly publishing practices within the context of doctoral study (Aitchison et al., 2010b; Matzler, 2022; Starke-Meyerring, 2011). To begin with, this paucity of research on scholarly publishing during doctoral study might be partly attributed to the primary emphasis of previous research on the broad geolinguistic and geopolitical contexts, and the relatively less attention to local social, cultural, and institutional contexts (Matzler, 2022). Second, although the institutionalisation of doctoral publication has been discussed and debated in the literature, institutional policies on doctoral publication and their potential influences on doctoral students' publishing practices and evolving identities have received scant research attention. The relationships between doctoral students' motives for and practices of scholarly publishing within the context of doctoral study have garnered even less attention. Third, because few studies have focused on scholarly publishing as nested within doctoral study, relatively little is known about specific challenges that doctoral students may face in their scholarly publishing efforts amidst competing demands from their doctoral studies, and strategies that they adopt to negotiate their scholarly publishing activities against such a backdrop (see, Lundell & Beach, 2003, for a similar trend in research on thesis writing). Fourth, even fewer studies have investigated how doctoral students cope with their dual identities as novice and expert researchers as they engage in scholarly publishing during their candidature.

Thus, drawing on a longitudinal study of Chinese nursing doctoral students' scholarly publishing experiences and practices, this book explores policies, practices, and identities related to doctoral publication, and possible connections between them. In doing so, the book aims to contribute to a more contextualised understanding of doctoral publication and provide implications for facilitating scholarly publishing during doctoral candidature.

1.1 Publishing During Doctoral Candidature

While doctoral publication per se, as noted above, has received relatively little attention, some studies focusing primarily on English as an additional language (EAL) researchers' scholarly publishing practices (e.g., Blakeslee, 1997; Casanave & Li, 2008; Flowerdew & Li, 2007; Li, 2005) and doctoral thesis writing (e.g., Belcher, 1994; Dong, 1996, 1998; Kamler & Thomson, 2006; Lundell & Beach, 2003) have touched upon scholarly publishing during doctoral candidature. These studies have yielded findings that may also hold implications for scholarly publishing during candidature. For example, some of the EAL researchers examined in previous studies are doctoral students, and some of the EAL researchers' motives, challenges, and strategies for scholarly publishing are shared by doctoral students. For this reason, drawing upon research on scholarly publishing during doctoral candidature as well as research on EAL researchers' scholarly publishing and doctoral thesis writing, I focus in this section on the motives, challenges, and strategies of doctoral students' scholarly publishing during their candidature.

Doctoral students' motives for scholarly publishing

As discussed earlier, doctoral students may have a multitude of motives for scholarly publishing. To begin with, there is evidence to suggest that publishing during doctoral candidature has been increasingly institutionalised as a graduation requirement or expectation for doctoral students across the world, such as in Hungary (Nagano & Spiczéné, 2018), Indonesia (Rochmyaningsih, March 9, 2012), Japan (Casanave,

2010; Gosden, 1995, 1996), Chinese mainland (Cargill et al., 2012; Li & Flowerdew, 2007), Taiwan (Huang, 2010, 2011, 2014), and the U.S. (Barbero, 2008). Li (2007, 2016) points out that doctoral science students at many universities in Chinese mainland have to publish in internationally indexed journals before they are allowed to graduate. Likewise, although only 12 out of the 70 mechanical engineering programmes in North America surveyed in Barbero's (2008) study "require" their doctoral students to publish one or two papers as partial fulfilment of the graduation requirements, another 52 "strongly encourage" their students to publish during candidature. Against this backdrop, fulfilling institutional graduation requirements may increasingly become a motive for doctoral students to publish during candidature.

In addition to meeting institutional publication requirements, publishing during doctoral candidature offers students opportunities to learn the ropes of the publishing game, especially through the reviewing process. Mizzi (2014) notes that publishing during candidature provides "the opportunity to receive and give mentorship, work on oral and written communication skills, organize ideas, network with established and emerging scholars, socialize with like-minded individuals, and learn of the publication process from start to finish" (p. 58). Specifically, the reviewing process has been found to help doctoral students improve their theses (Hartley & Betts, 2009; Kamler, 2008; Robins & Kanowski, 2008) and develop their scholarly publishing skills (Mizzi, 2014; Paré, 2010). Kamler (2008), for example, observes that the reviewing process in scholarly publishing "has clear benefits for the thesis in providing a usable, public critique" (p. 290). Additionally, Robins and Kanowski (2008) have identified other benefits of the reviewing process, such as "exposing students to a wider community within their research domain, introducing new perspectives, and driving improvement in students' analytical and writing skills" (p. 11). Thus, publishing during doctoral candidature can play a pivotal role in enhancing doctoral students' scholarly publishing skills. As Mizzi (2014) states, "While they may successfully complete their dissertations, without any publications they [doctoral students] may still lack the skills to publish in academic contexts" (p. 55).

Further, research has shown that publishing during doctoral candidature can boost doctoral students' job prospects (Casanave, 2010; Kwan, 2010, 2013; McGrail et al., 2006; Paré, 2010; Watts, 2012) and future research productivity (Hartley & Betts, 2009; Kamler, 2008; Weidman & Stein, 2003; Williamson & Cable, 2003). With both nations and institutions competing fiercely for productive young and established researchers to enhance their research productivity and profile (Cuthbert & Spark, 2008; Lee & Kamler, 2008; Sinclair et al., 2014), doctoral students' publication track records are playing an increasingly important role in securing post-doctoral employment, particularly research employment. In a survey of 58 postgraduate students, Hartley and Betts (2009) found that publications during candidature bolstered the students' chances of landing a job. Similarly, Sinclair et al. (2014) have noted that "[c]andidates completing doctorates with some publications are better placed for future employment" (p. 1977). Moreover, Kamler (2008) points out that "if students publish in their formative years, they are more likely to do so as established academics or informed professionals in their chosen fields of practice" (p. 292).

In summary, doctoral students may have a range of motives for publishing during candidature, including learning the trade of scholarly publishing, meeting the institutional graduation requirements, and preparing for their future careers. These motives suggest that scholarly publishing during doctoral candidature is a high-stakes activity. As I will illustrate below, as a high-stakes activity, scholarly publishing tends to pose great challenges to doctoral students.

Doctoral students' challenges in scholarly publishing

As noted above, the challenges encountered by doctoral students attempting to publish during candidature revolve around the competing demands of doctoral study within a tight timeframe and doctoral students' fledgling scholarly abilities. The former is concerned mainly with the time constraints that doctoral students are often under in accomplishing the multiple, and often competing, activities of doctoral study, especially scholarly publishing during doctoral candidature and timely completion of a thesis (Casanave, 2010; Hartley & Betts, 2009; Lee & Aitchison, 2011; Lundell & Beach, 2003; Mizzi, 2014). The latter relates to difficulties and challenges arising from the gaps between doctoral students' still developing scholarly abilities and the expert skills and knowledge needed for successful scholarly publishing (Aitchison & Lee, 2006; Caffarella & Barnett, 2000; Can & Walker, 2011; Mizzi, 2014). As Sinclair et al. (2014) point out, doctoral students' role as student researchers and the expectations for them to publish like expert researchers are paradoxical.

A major challenge for doctoral students seeking to publish during candidature is to juggle multiple, and often competing, demands within a tight timeframe (Lee & Aitchison, 2011). While writing for publication is a time-consuming activity itself (Pasco, 2009; Watts, 2012), doctoral students have to deal with other tasks and responsibilities at the same time, such as teaching, research, presenting at conferences, departmental or institutional administrative tasks, and family responsibilities (Casanave, 2010; Lundell & Beach, 2003; Mizzi, 2014). As a result, they may lead "packed and pressured lives" and face "impossible circumstances" in their scholarly publishing endeavours (Casanave, 2010, p. 48). The doctoral students in Beauchamp et al.'s (2009) study, for instance, frequently mentioned tensions and frustrations related to "lack of time or interference of other activities" (p. 273).

In particular, scholarly publishing and timely completion of theses may compete against each other for doctoral students' limited time (Hartley & Betts, 2009; Lundell & Beach, 2003; Watts, 2012). Lee and Aitchison (2011), for example, observe that "for students under pressure to complete their doctoral studies in a timely fashion and produce a dissertation as well as publications en route, there are very real challenges concerning how to manage writing multiple related texts" (p. 69). Apart from competing for time, thesis writing and scholarly publishing tend to follow different conventions and norms, which may give rise to contradictions or systemic conflicts (Lundell & Beach, 2003; Simpson, 2013). For example, Paulo, the doctoral student in Simpson's (2013) study, came across "a systemic conflict" between his thesis writing and scholarly publishing, which is considered to be one of the "systemic contradictions between graduate school expectations and scientific writing practices" (p. 243). Similarly, Lundell and Beach (2003) found in their study that "participants experienced a double bind arising from the contradiction between writing according to the genre rules of the Graduate School and department systems and writing for publication and conference papers valued in the job market system" (p. 503).

In addition to time pressure and competing demands and expectations, doctoral students may find themselves underprepared for scholarly publishing given their role as student and fledgling researchers and the dearth of support that they may receive (Aitchison & Lee, 2006; Caffarella & Barnett, 2000; Can & Walker, 2011). Mizzi (2014) notes that doctoral students may "fee[l] inadequate to contribute anything meaningful to the literature" (p. 58). For this reason, some scholars have cautioned that scholarly publishing during doctoral candidature may cause anxiety, damage self-confidence, or lead to premature publishing (Clowes & Shefer, 2013; Paré, 2010; Pasco, 2009). As Paré (2010) points out, "the anxiety to publish can hamper rather than help students" (p. 30). Likewise, premature publishing runs the risk of "short-circuiting or abbreviating the potentially enriching experience of writing-to-learn and the rhetorical chance-taking that leads to innovation and discovery" (Paré, 2010, p. 37). Further, there seem to be disciplinary differences in terms of doctoral students' preparedness for scholarly publishing. Research has shown that doctoral students in the humanities and social sciences tend to be less prepared than their counterparts in the sciences (Kamler, 2008; Lee & Kamler, 2008).

To sum up, doctoral students seeking to publish during candidature may encounter challenges that are inherent in doctoral education and that stem from their dual identities as student and as expert researchers. To publish successfully, they need strategies to cope with these challenges. In the next section, I survey and discuss several such strategies found in the literature.

Doctoral students' strategies for scholarly publishing

Several strategies have been suggested in the literature to facilitate doctoral students' attempts to publish during candidature, including receiving pedagogical support (Aitchison et al., 2010b; Cotterall, 2011; Kwan, 2010, 2013; Lee & Kamler, 2008; Li, 2016; Li & Flowerdew, 2007; Morss & Murray, 2001), seeking mentoring from supervisors or other experienced researchers (Casanave, 1998; Cho, 2004; Connor, 1999; Hasrati, 2013; Lee & Roth, 2003; Li, 2005), and adopting the article-compilation thesis format (Dong, 1996, 1998; Lee, 2010; Robins & Kanowski, 2008).

Pedagogical support for scholarly publishing has been increasingly recognised as a useful strategy to foster doctoral students' scholarly publishing skills and to boost their scholarly publishing outputs (Aitchison et al., 2010b; Cotterall, 2011; Kwan, 2010, 2013; Lee & Kamler, 2008; Li, 2016; Li & Flowerdew, 2007; Morss & Murray, 2001). Various forms of pedagogical intervention have been proposed to enhance doctoral students' abilities to publish, such as seminars, workshops, writing groups, and writing courses (Aitchison et al., 2010b; Kamler & Thomson, 2006). While all of these interventions have been found effective in boosting researchers' publication output, regular and ongoing support has been deemed most effective (McGrail et al., 2006). However, it should be noted that although there have been calls for pedagogical support for scholarly publishing for a long time, it started to garner research attention only recently (Kamler & Thomson, 2006; Lee & Kamler, 2008; Starke-Meyerring, 2011). Meanwhile, traditional or existing academic writing courses tend to cover only general and basic writing skills, which are inadequate to help doctoral students to navigate the complex scholarly publishing activities (Flowerdew, 2015; Kwan, 2010, 2013) because scholarly publishing "involves not only writing but also strategic conception of research ideas, as well as output planning and management" (Kwan, 2013, p. 210). Therefore, there is limited empirical evidence regarding whether and what types of instruction are available and effective in improving doctoral students' scholarly publishing abilities (Kwan, 2010, 2013; Watts, 2012). As Aitchison et al. (2010a) observe, "universities are often happy that their research students are publishing, but often not skillful in recognizing the pedagogical work involved in bringing students into a productive relationship with the practices of publication" (pp. 2–3).

Another strategy that doctoral students can utilise to bolster their scholarly publishing is seeking mentoring from their supervisors and other experienced researchers, particularly through coauthoring with them (Casanave, 1998; Connor, 1999; Hasrati, 2013; Lee & Roth, 2003; Matzler, 2022). Coauthoring with supervisors is considered to be one of the "multiple ways to foster doctoral publication" (Kamler, 2008, p. 285). For example, Mr. Kubo and Dr. Iwahara, two young Japanese researchers in Casanave's (1998) study, regarded their coauthoring experiences with their supervisors during their doctoral studies in the U.S. as "[o]ne of the most valuable experiences" (p. 184) and "perhaps the most influential learning experience" (p. 185), respectively. In addition, coauthoring with supervisors can help doctoral students cope with anxiety, rejections, and harsh criticisms that are often associated with scholarly publishing (Kamler, 2008; Pasco, 2009). As Kamler (2008) notes, coauthoring with supervisors can help doctoral students "move through the struggles and anxieties of publishing" and learn "how to be robust in the face of rejection and ongoing revision" (p. 292). Further, through coauthoring with their supervisors, doctoral students can familiarise themselves not only with the discursive practices of English scholarly writing but also with the values, beliefs, ideologies and even ways of being that underpin the discourse community. For example, Fei, a Chinese doctoral student in Li's (2005) study, learned not only "ways of writing" but also "ways of being" (p. 166) from his experiences of coauthoring three journal articles with his supervisor.

However, despite the usefulness of mentoring from supervisors through coauthoring, whether and to what extent all doctoral students can receive such mentoring from their supervisors remains "a moot point" (Dinham & Scott, 2001, p. 46). First, supervisors and doctoral students may have different views and expectations regarding the amount and/or type of assistance that the former should provide to the latter. In particular, while some supervisors may consider it part of their job to help their doctoral students publish, others may not think so (Aitchison et al., 2012; Li, 2016). Research has found that while supervisors tend to provide general support or feedback, doctoral students are inclined to need detailed, specific, and ongoing support (Can & Walker, 2011; Florence & Yore, 2004; Hanauer & Englander, 2013; Lei & Hu, 2015). Second, research has also documented supervisors' constrained ability to provide certain types of assistance in scholarly publishing, such as language support (Bazerman, 2009; Kwan, 2010, 2013; Lei & Hu, 2015; Li & Flowerdew, 2007; Paré, 2010; Strauss et al., 2003). Third, supervisors may find it difficult to articulate the norms and conventions because they are often tacit or occluded (Bazerman, 2009; Blakeslee, 1997; Kwan, 2010, 2013; Paré et al., 2011; Starke-Meyerring, 2011). Paré et al. (2011), for example, point out that while supervisors may have no problems performing "the knowledge-making practices of their research communities" (p. 223), they may find it difficult to enunciate them.

A third strategy recommended in the literature to help doctoral students publish during candidature is adopting the article-compilation thesis format (Cuthbert & Spark, 2008; Dong, 1996; Lee, 2010; Powell, 2004; Robins & Kanowski, 2008). As doctoral students taking the traditional thesis route often publish their theses or part of their theses *after* rather than *during* their candidature, one benefit of the article-compilation thesis route is that it can help "secure both degree completions and increased publications simultaneously" (Cuthbert & Spark, 2008, p. 79). Additionally, taking the article-compilation thesis route can also resolve or ameliorate the difficulty of transforming theses into journal articles, which has been identified as "a systematic conflict" (Simpson, 2013, p. 243) or "a double bind arising from the contradiction between writing according to the genre rules of the Graduate School and department systems and writing for publications and conference papers" (Lundell & Beach, 2003, p. 503).

Despite its potential for enhancing doctoral students' scholarly publishing during candidature, however, this strategy also has several limitations. For one thing, despite its increasing popularity, the article-compilation thesis format may not be accepted in some institutions or even known in some places (Kwan, 2013; Powell, 2004). For another, it would require strategic planning and management of thesis and manuscript writing to successfully implement the strategy (Kwan, 2010, 2013; Lee & Aitchison, 2011), such as how to design and develop publications that have an adequate scope for a doctoral thesis and how to make the publications a coherent thesis. Kwan (2010), for example, points out that "to produce a thesis following the article compilation (AC) format" entails aligning the activities of conducting research, writing up the thesis, and publishing (p. 59).

It is clear that although previous research has yielded valuable insights into publishing during doctoral candidature, we still know relatively little about policies, practices, identities, and their connections pertaining to it. There is thus a need for more research focusing specifically on policies, practices, and identities surrounding doctoral publication.

1.2 Overview of the Research

This book seeks to bring together policies, practices, identities, and their connections pertaining to doctoral publication through an in-depth longitudinal study of doctoral students' scholarly publishing endeavours. Although a small body of research has addressed each of these issues, few studies have attempted to deal with them together. Informed by the theoretical frameworks of neoliberalism and activity theory, it examines doctoral students' scholarly publishing activities within the context of their doctoral studies, and demonstrates how policies, practices, and identities intersect with each other and how policies may shape doctoral students' publishing practices and evolving identities.

Specifically, this book unveils neoliberal ideologies in institutional policies on doctoral publication and identifies misalignments between institutional policies and stakeholder perspectives. It also examines doctoral students' scholarly publishing practices in the context of their busy doctoral studies and shows how they manage to have their work published amid competing demands from their doctoral studies. These findings indicate that institutional publication policies have a great bearing on their publishing practices. Additionally, the book explores doctoral students' evolving identities in their scholarly publishing endeavours. It demonstrates the duality of their identities—novice and expert researchers—as evidenced by their challenges in applying conceptual tools for scholarly publishing and their skilful leveraging of mediating resources to cope with the challenges, showing that doctoral publication entails both constraints and affordances.

To grapple with the issues delineated above, this study adopted a multiple-case study design (Yin, 2009) and examined six Chinese nursing doctoral students' scholarly publishing experiences and practices within the context of their doctoral studies. The present study was conducted in a nursing doctoral programme at a major comprehensive university in Chinese mainland. The Nursing Department is one of the five departments of the School of Medicine, and offers programmes at the associate, baccalaureate, master's, and doctoral levels. It was among the earliest to offer master's programmes in nursing science in Chinese mainland. Its nursing doctoral programme commenced in the middle 2000s and was among the first ten nursing doctoral programmes in Chinese mainland. The nursing doctoral programme is a three-year research doctorate. The Nursing Department also offers a joint-degrees programme in partnership with an English-medium university outside Chinese mainland (hereafter the partner university).[1] Although the partner university offers both professional (D.H.Sc., Doctor of Health Science) and research (Ph.D., Doctor of Philosophy) doctoral degrees in nursing science, the joint-degrees programme is a research doctorate. Students in the joint-degrees programme are required to fulfill the graduation requirements of both universities to be awarded both degrees, including coursework prescribed by both universities, the focal university's publication requirements, and a thesis in Chinese for the focal university and an English translation of the thesis for the partner university.

Six doctoral students in the Nursing Department were selected purposefully to generate the richest possible information about the issues under study (Patton, 2002). While four students (Dong, Fang, Wei, and Xiao; all names used in this book are pseudonyms) were enrolled in the nursing doctoral programme, two students (Cui and Liang) were among the first cohort of the joint-degrees programme. Five doctoral

---

[1] Information on the partner university is not provided for the sake of anonymity.

1.2 Overview of the Research

students were just enrolled in the doctoral programmes at the beginning of this study, while one student (Wei) was one year into her doctoral study. Cui, Liang, Wei, and Xiao were under the supervision of Professor Liu, whereas Dong and Fang were supervised by Professor Wu. Both professors were invited to participate in this study through their doctoral students. However, while Professor Liu agreed to participate, Professor Wu declined my invitation because of her busy schedule and multiple commitments.

To address the research questions, I collected different types of data from multiple sources (see Table 1.1), including in-depth interviews with the students and their supervisor; the students' manuscripts and thesis drafts, course assignments (if relevant and available), and related artefacts; policy documents and artefacts regarding the university, the school of medicine, the university's doctoral programmes, the focal Ph.D. programme, and the joint-degrees programme; and text-based interviews with the doctoral students about their rationales for some discursive practices in their manuscripts, their views on selected comments on their manuscripts, and their perceived reasons for selected revisions made by themselves and others. The collection of different types of data from multiple sources constituted an attempt to triangulate the data and enhance the trustworthiness of the findings derived from this study (Lincoln & Guba, 1985; Merriam, 1998; Miles & Huberman, 1994).

The data were analysed following Yamagata-Lynch's (2007, 2010) approach, which comprises a thematic analysis and an activity systems analysis. The purpose of the thematic analysis was to identify themes or issues and relationships among them for further exploration from an activity theory perspective (see Sect. 2.3). To that end, I followed general principles informed by grounded theory (Charmaz, 2006) in analysing the data. Thus, my thematic analysis consisted of three phases, namely, initial coding, focused coding, and axial coding. Following Yamagata-Lynch's (2007, 2010) approach to activity systems analysis, my activity systems analysis included three steps, identifying the unit of analysis, bounded systems, and activity settings; constructing the networks of activity systems; and delineating the contradictions within and between activity systems. Although my analysis at each stage was divided into three phases, the whole process was recursive, and in the process, I went back and forth between different phases of analysis, modifying and refining the emerging codes.

Finally, I drew upon the results of both the thematic analysis and the activity systems analysis to identify contradictions concerning the doctoral students' scholarly publishing activity. Specifically, I went back and forth iteratively between the results of the thematic analysis and those of the activity systems analysis to map them onto one another (Yamagata-Lynch, 2007, 2010). In so doing, I was able to gain an insight into the systemic causes of the doctoral students' challenges for scholarly publishing, possible rationales for their coping strategies, and potential consequences of their coping strategies both for themselves and for the scholarly publishing activity, thus revealing possible connections between policies, practices, and identities related to doctoral publication.

Table 1.1 A summary of the data collection methods and the data collected

Method	Source and type of data

In-depth interviews	✓ Interviews (including face-to-face, email, and QQ ones[2]) with student participants about
	  • their experience and training in English and Chinese (academic) writing
	  • their prior experiences, knowledge, and skills concerning writing and academic writing
	  • their views on scholarly writing and publishing
	  • their views on the university's publication requirements
	  • their writing and publishing processes
	  • their encountered difficulties and challenges in scholarly publishing
	  • sources and types of help in their scholarly publishing activities
	✓ Interview with the supervisor about
	  • her perceptions about the scholarly publishing abilities of the doctoral students in the nursing department
	  • her views on the university's publication requirements
	  • difficulties and challenges her doctoral students often face in their scholarly publishing efforts
	  • strategies her students often employ to cope with the difficulties and challenges

Artifacts and documents collection	✓ Brochures, booklets, and online documents about
	  • the focal university, the partner university, the school of medicine, the nursing department (e.g., history, mission statements)
	  • the doctoral programme, and the joint-degrees programme (e.g., the programme structure, and requirements and regulations about coursework, publication, thesis research)
	  • journals' instructions for authors
	✓ Written texts
	  • drafts, revisions, and final drafts of their manuscripts, theses, and course assignments
	  • supervisor's comments on the drafts
	  • comments from others, if any, on the drafts
	  • editors' and reviewers' comments on their manuscripts
	  • student participants' responses to various comments
	  • correspondence with journal editors

Text-based interviews	✓ Text-based interviews with student participants about
	  • their rationales for some discursive practice in their manuscripts
	  • their views on selected comments on their manuscripts and on their revisions
	  • their perceived reasons for some selected revisions made by themselves and others

I utilised several strategies to improve the trustworthiness of the findings of the present study. First, the prolonged engagement with the participants provided opportunities for me to get to know them personally, establish trust with them, understand their way of doing things in relation to scholarly writing and publishing, and clarify

---

[2] QQ or Tencent QQ is an instant messaging software service developed by the Chinese company Tencent Holdings Limited. It is widely used for voice and video chat in Chinese mainland.

things that might not have been possible otherwise. Second, as mentioned earlier, this study drew upon different types of data from multiple sources, which could provide rich and textured evidence and thus lend more confidence to the findings obtained in the study. Together with prolonged engagement, such triangulation led to not only a 'thick description' (Geertz, 1973) but also an elucidation of multiple perspectives. Third, I maintained a conscious awareness of my positionality in the present study and remained reflexive throughout the whole research in the hope that my role in the research would not undermine but enhance the trustworthiness of the findings. Finally, I sent the results of my activity systems analyses to three student participants (Cui, Dong, Liang) and asked them to check their accuracy for me, a strategy that is seen by Lincoln and Guba (1985) as "the most critical technique for establishing credibility" (p. 314). These strategies together have helped to ensure the trustworthiness of the findings derived from the study.

1.3 Organisation of the Book

This book consists of six chapters. Chapter 2 introduces the theoretical perspectives underpinning this research. It first argues for an overarching conceptualisation of doctoral publication as a sociopolitical practice. Following that, it delineates in turn neoliberal perspectives and activity theory perspectives on doctoral publication. The chapter closes with some concluding remarks on the implications of these theoretical perspectives for this research.

Chapter 3 explores institutional policies on doctoral publication and supervisor and doctoral student perspectives on those policies. In analysing the focal university's requirements and rewards schemes for doctoral publication, this chapter reveals that the institutional policies subscribe to neoliberal ideologies, endorse market rationalities, and privilege managerial over professional values and practices. Then the chapter details supervisor and student perspectives on the institutional requirements and rewards schemes for doctoral publication, showing that the supervisor and doctoral students prioritise internal motivations over external material and symbolic rewards for publishing. The next section of the chapter discusses (mis)alignments between institutional policies and stakeholder perspectives on doctoral publication. This chapter concludes with a critique of the (mis)alignments between institutional policies and stakeholder perspectives, and a discussion of the potential impacts of the (mis)alignments on doctoral students' publishing practices and evolving identities. Part of the data reported in this chapter were originally published in *Studies in Continuing Education* (Lei, 2021).

Chapter 4 examines doctoral publication practices by grappling with the competing demands on doctoral students and the coping strategies they adopted to cope with the demands. It illustrates the competing demands and time pressure encountered by doctoral students in their scholarly publishing efforts. An activity theory analysis of these challenges reveals a contradiction concerning developing the doctoral students into fully-fledged knowledge producers while timely graduating them and having their knowledge contributions published. This primary contradiction was manifested in the time pressure faced by the doctoral students in meeting the university's publication requirements and in the less-than-desirable managerial roles played by the university and supervisors. The doctoral students adopted two main strategies to cope with those challenges—boundary crossing through starting early and refashioning the scholarly publishing activity through orchestrating one's research and publication with those of others. The university and supervisor played primarily managerial roles in doctoral students' scholarly publishing activities. Finally, the chapter concludes by discussing these findings with reference to activity theory and the literature on scholarly publishing. Part of the data reported in this chapter were published in *TESOL Quarterly* (Lei, 2019).

Focusing on doctoral students' evolving and dual identities, Chap. 5 looks into the conceptual tools and the mediating resources they employed in their scholarly publishing endeavours. It sketches out the challenges faced by doctoral students in applying conceptual tools (e.g., language, and rules governing scholarly publishing) for scholarly publishing. From an activity theory perspective, these challenges were a manifestation of the doctoral students' developing, but still limited grasp and use of some conceptual tools needed for successful scholarly publishing, which was in turn a reflection of the doctoral students' dual roles as novice and expert researchers in their scholarly publishing efforts. The doctoral students employed various mediating resources to tackle the contradiction, and their employment of the mediating resources impinged not only on the scholarly publishing activity system but also on themselves as scholarly writers. Following that, the chapter discusses the constraints and affordances of doctoral publication. Finally, the findings of this chapter are discussed with reference to activity theory and the extant literature on doctoral publication and identities. Part of the data reported in this chapter were originally published in *English for Specific Purposes*, co-authored with Guangwei Hu (Lei & Hu, 2019).

Chapter 6 brings together the findings from Chaps. 3 to 5, foregrounding the connections between policies, practices, and identities pertaining to doctoral publication. In bringing to the fore the connections between policies, practices, and identities, the chapter proposes a situated conceptualisation of doctoral publication as a dynamically evolving and chronotopically laminated activity and argues for the need to adopt a pragmatic approach to it. Finally, the chapter concludes by addressing the implications of this research for further research, theory, policy, and pedagogy.

References

Aitchison, C., Catterall, J., Ross, P., & Burgin, S. (2012). 'Tough love and tears': Learning doctoral writing in the sciences. *Higher Education Research & Development, 31*, 435–447. https://doi.org/10.1080/07294360.2011.559195

Aitchison, C., Kamler, B., & Lee, A. (2010a). Introduction: Why publishing pedagogies? In C. Aitchison, B. Kamler, & A. Lee (Eds.), *Publishing pedagogies for the doctorate and beyond* (pp. 1–11). Routledge.

References

Aitchison, C., Kamler, B., & Lee, A. (2010b). *Publishing pedagogies for the doctorate and beyond.* Routledge.

Aitchison, C., & Lee, A. (2006). Research writing: Problems and pedagogies. *Teaching in Higher Education, 11*, 265–278. https://doi.org/10.1080/13562510600680574

Barbero, E. J. (2008). Journal paper requirement for PhD graduation. *Latin American and Caribbean Journal of Engineering Education, 2*, 51–53.

Bardi, M. (2015). Learning the practice of scholarly publication in English—A Romanian perspective. *English for Specific Purposes, 37*, 98–111. https://doi.org/10.1016/j.esp.2014.08.002

Bazerman, C. (2009). Genre and cognitive development: Beyond writing to learn. In C. Bazerman, A. Bonin, & D. Figueiredo (Eds.), *Genre in a changing world* (pp. 279–294). The WAC Clearinghouse.

Beauchamp, C., Jazvac-Martek, M., & McAlpine, L. (2009). Studying doctoral education: Using activity theory to shape methodological tools. *Innovations in Education and Teaching International, 46*, 265–277. https://doi.org/10.1080/14703290903068839

Becher, T., & Trowler, P. R. (2001). *Academic tribes and territories: Intellectual enquiry and the culture of disciplines* (2nd ed.). Open University Press.

Belcher, D. (1994). The apprenticeship approach to advanced academic literacy: Graduate students and their mentors. *English for Specific Purposes, 13*, 23–34. https://doi.org/10.1016/0889-4906(94)90022-1

Blakeslee, A. M. (1997). Activity, context, interaction, and authority. *Journal of Business and Technical Communication, 11*, 125–169. https://doi.org/10.1177/1050651997011002001

Caffarella, R. S., & Barnett, B. G. (2000). Teaching doctoral students to become scholarly writers: The importance of giving and receiving critiques. *Studies in Higher Education, 25*, 39–52. https://doi.org/10.1080/030750700116000

Can, G., & Walker, A. (2011). A model for doctoral students' perceptions and attitudes toward written feedback for academic writing. *Research in Higher Education, 52*, 508–536. https://doi.org/10.1007/s11162-010-9204-1

Cargill, M., O'Connor, P., & Li, Y. (2012). Educating Chinese scientists to write for international journals: Addressing the divide between science and technology education and English language teaching. *English for Specific Purposes, 31*, 60–69. https://doi.org/10.1016/j.esp.2011.05.003

Casanave, C. P. (1998). Transitions: The balancing act of bilingual academics. *Journal of Second Language Writing, 12*, 175–203. https://doi.org/10.1016/S1060-3743(98)90012-1

Casanave, C. P. (2010). Dovetailing under impossible circumstances. In C. Aitchison, B. Kamler, & A. Lee (Eds.), *Publishing pedagogies for the doctorate and beyond* (pp. 47–63). Routledge.

Casanave, C. P., & Li, X. M. (Eds.). (2008). *Learning the literacy practices of graduate school: Insiders' reflections on academic enculturation.* University of Michigan Press.

Charmaz, K. (2006). *Constructing grounded theory: A practical guide through qualitative analysis.* Sage.

Cho, S. (2004). Challenges of entering discourse communities through publishing in English: Perspectives of nonnative-speaking doctoral students in the United States of America. *Journal of Language, Identity & Education, 3*, 47–72. https://doi.org/10.1207/s15327701jlie0301_3

Clowes, L., & Shefer, T. (2013). "It's not a simple thing, co-publishing": Challenges of co-authorship between supervisors and students in South African higher educational contexts. *Africa Education Review, 10*, 32–47. https://doi.org/10.1080/18146627.2013.786865

Connor, U. (1999). Learning to write academic prose in a second language: A literacy autobiography. In G. Braine (Ed.), *Non-native educators in English language teaching* (pp. 29–42). Lawrence Erlbaum.

Cotterall, S. (2011). Doctoral students writing: Where's the pedagogy? *Teaching in Higher Education, 16*, 413–425. https://doi.org/10.1080/13562517.2011.560381

Cuthbert, D., & Spark, C. (2008). Getting a GRiP: Examining the outcomes of a pilot program to support graduate research students in writing for publication. *Studies in Higher Education, 33*, 77–88. https://doi.org/10.1080/03075070701794841

Dinham, S., & Scott, C. (2001). The experience of disseminating the results of doctoral research. *Journal of Further and Higher Education, 25*, 45–55. https://doi.org/10.1080/03098770200 30498

Dong, Y. R. (1996). Learning how to use citations for knowledge transformation: Non-native doctoral students' dissertation writing in science. *Research in the Teaching of English, 30*, 428–457.

Dong, Y. R. (1998). Non-native graduate students' thesis/dissertation writing in science: Self-reports by students and their advisors from two U.S. institutions. *English for Specific Purposes, 17*, 369–390. https://doi.org/10.1016/s0889-4906(97)00054-9

Florence, M. K., & Yore, L. D. (2004). Learning to write like a scientist: Coauthoring as an enculturation task. *Journal of Research in Science Teaching, 41*, 637–668. https://doi.org/10.1002/tea.20015

Flowerdew, J. (2015). Some thoughts on English for Research Publication Purposes (ERPP) and related issues. *Language Teaching, 48*, 250–262. https://doi.org/10.1017/S0261444812000523

Flowerdew, J., & Habibie, P. (2022). *Introducing English for research publication purposes*. Routledge.

Flowerdew, J., & Li, Y. (2007). Language re-use among Chinese apprentice scientists writing for publication. *Applied Linguistics, 28*, 440–465. https://doi.org/10.1093/applin/amm031

Geertz, C. (1973). *The interpretation of cultures: Selected essays*. Basic Books.

Gosden, H. (1995). Success in research article writing and revision: A social constructionist perspective. *English for Specific Purposes, 14*, 37–57. https://doi.org/10.1016/0889-4906(94)000 22-6

Gosden, H. (1996). Verbal reports of Japanese novices' research writing practices in English. *Journal of Second Language Writing, 5*, 109–128. https://doi.org/10.1016/s1060-3743(96)90021-1

Hanauer, D. I., & Englander, K. (2013). *Scientific writing in a second language*. Parlor Press.

Hartley, J., & Betts, L. (2009). Publishing before the thesis: 58 postgraduate views. *Higher Education Review, 41*, 29–44.

Hasrati, M. (2013). Material and credentialing incentives as symbolic violence: Local engagement and global participation through joint publication. *Journal of Business and Technical Communication, 27*, 154–179. https://doi.org/10.1177/1050651912468886

Huang, J. C. (2010). Publishing and learning writing for publication in English: Perspectives of NNES PhD students in science. *Journal of English for Academic Purposes, 9*, 33–44. https://doi.org/10.1016/j.jeap.2009.10.001

Huang, J. C. (2011). Attitudes of Taiwanese scholars toward English and Chinese as languages of publication. *Asia Pacific Journal of Education, 31*, 115–128. https://doi.org/10.1080/02188791. 2011.566983

Huang, J. C. (2014). Learning to write for publication in English through genre-based pedagogy: A case in Taiwan. *System, 45*, 175–186. https://doi.org/10.1016/j.system.2014.05.010

Kamler, B. (2008). Rethinking doctoral publication practices: Writing from and beyond the thesis. *Studies in Higher Education, 33*, 283–294. https://doi.org/10.1080/03075070802049236

Kamler, B., & Thomson, P. (2006). *Helping doctoral students write: Pedagogies for supervision*. Routledge.

Kwan, B. S. C. (2010). An investigation of instruction in research publishing offered in doctoral programs: The Hong Kong case. *Higher Education, 59*, 55–68. https://doi.org/10.1007/s10734-009-9233-x

Kwan, B. S. C. (2013). Facilitating novice researchers in project publishing during the doctoral years and beyond: A Hong Kong-based study. *Studies in Higher Education, 38*, 207–225. https://doi.org/10.1080/03075079.2011.576755

Lee, A. (2010). When the aticle is the dissertation: Pedagogies for a PhD by publication. In C. Aitchison, B. Kamler, & A. Lee (Eds.), *Publishing pedagogies for the doctorate and beyond* (pp. 12–29). Routledge.

References

Lee, A., & Aitchison, C. (2011). Working with tensions: Writing for publication during your doctorate. In T. S. Rocco & T. Hatcher (Eds.), *The handbook of scholarly writing and publishing* (pp. 62–74). Jossey Bass.

Lee, A., & Kamler, B. (2008). Bringing pedagogy to doctoral publishing. *Teaching in Higher Education, 13*, 511–523. https://doi.org/10.1080/13562510802334723

Lee, S., & Roth, W.-M. (2003). Becoming and belonging: Learning qualitative research through legitimate peripheral participation. *Forum: Qualitative Social Research, 4*, Art. 35. http://nbn-resolving.de/urn:nbn:de:0114-fqs0302355

Lei, J. (2019). Publishing during doctoral candidature from an activity theory perspective: The case of four Chinese nursing doctoral students. *TESOL Quarterly, 53*, 655–684. https://doi.org/10.1002/tesq.501

Lei, J. (2021). Neoliberal ideologies in a Chinese university's requirements and rewards schemes for doctoral publication. *Studies in Continuing Education, 43*, 68–85. https://doi.org/10.1080/0158037X.2019.1672638

Lei, J., & Hu, G. (2015). Apprenticeship in scholarly publishing: A student perspective on doctoral supervisors' roles. *Publications, 3*, 27–42. https://doi.org/10.3390/publications3010027

Lei, J., & Hu, G. (2019). Doctoral candidates' dual role as student and expert scholarly writer: An activity theory perspective. *English for Specific Purposes, 54*, 62–74. https://doi.org/10.1016/j.esp.2018.12.003

Li, Y. (2005). Multidimensional enculturation: The case of an EFL Chinese doctoral student. *Journal of Asian Pacific Communication, 15*, 153–170. https://doi.org/10.1075/japc.15.1.10li

Li, Y. (2007). Apprentice scholarly writing in a community of practice: An interview of an NNES graduate student writing a research article. *TESOL Quarterly, 41*, 55–79. https://doi.org/10.1002/j.1545-7249.2007.tb00040.x

Li, Y. (2016). "Publish SCI papers or no degree": Practices of Chinese doctoral supervisors in response to the publication pressure on science students. *Asia Pacific Journal of Education, 36*, 545–558. https://doi.org/10.1080/02188791.2015.1005050

Li, Y., & Flowerdew, J. (2007). Shaping Chinese novice scientists' manuscripts for publication. *Journal of Second Language Writing, 16*, 100–117. https://doi.org/10.1016/j.jslw.2007.05.001

Lillis, T., & Curry, M. J. (2010). *Academic writing in a global context: The politics and practices of publishing in English*. Routledge.

Lincoln, Y. S., & Guba, E. G. (1985). *Naturalistic inquiry*. Sage.

Lundell, D. B., & Beach, R. (2003). Dissertation writers' negotiations with competing activity systems. In C. Bazerman & D. Russell (Eds.), *Writing selves/Writing societies* (pp. 483–514). The WAC Clearinghouse.

Matzler, P. P. (2022). *Mentoring and co-writing for research publication purposes: Interaction and text development in doctoral supervision*. Routledge.

McGrail, M. R., Rickard, C. M., & Jones, R. (2006). Publish or perish: A systematic review of interventions to increase academic publication rates. *Higher Education Research & Development, 25*, 19–35. https://doi.org/10.1080/07294360500453053

Merriam, S. B. (1998). *Qualitative research and case study applications in education*. Jossey-Bass.

Miles, M. B., & Huberman, A. M. (1994). *Qualitative data analysis: An expanded sourcebook* (2nd ed.). Sage.

Mizzi, R. C. (2014). Writing realities: An exploration of drawbacks and benefits of publishing while enrolled in a doctoral program. *New Horizons in Adult Education and Human Resource Development, 26*, 54–59. https://doi.org/10.1002/nha3.20063

Morss, K., & Murray, R. (2001). Researching academic writing within a structured programme: Insights and outcomes. *Studies in Higher Education, 26*, 35–52. https://doi.org/10.1080/03075070020030706

Nagano, R. L., & Spiczéné, B. (2018). PhD publication requirements and practices: A multidisciplinary case study of a Hungarian university. In M. Curry & T. Lillis (Eds.), *Global academic publishing: Policies, perspectives, and pedagogies* (pp. 37–48). Multilingual Matters.

Nerad, M. (2020). Doctoral education worldwide: Three decades of change. In M. Yudkevich, P. Altbach, & H. de Wit (Eds.), *Trends and issues in doctoral education: A global perspective* (pp. 33–45). Sage.

Paré, A. (2010). Slow the presses: Concerns for premature publication. In C. Aitchison, B. Kamler, & A. Lee (Eds.), *Publishing pedagogies for the doctorate and beyond* (pp. 30–46). Routledge.

Paré, A., Starke-Meyerring, D., & McAlpine, L. (2011). Knowledge and identity work in the supervision of doctoral student writing: Shaping rhetorical subjects. In D. Starke-Meyerring, A. Paré, N. Artemeva, M. Horne, & L. Yousoubova (Eds.), *Writing in knowledge societies* (pp. 215–236). Parlor Press and WAC Clearinghouse.

Pasco, A. H. (2009). Should graduate students publish? *Journal of Scholarly Publishing, 40*, 231–240.

Patton, M. Q. (2002). *Qualitative research and evaluation methods*. Sage.

Powell, S. (2004). *Award of the PhD by published work in the UK*. UK Council for Graduate Education.

Raddon, A. E. (2011). A changing environment: Narratives of learning about research. *International Journal for Researcher Development, 2*, 26–45. https://doi.org/10.1108/17597511111178005

Robins, L., & Kanowski, P. (2008). PhD by publication: A student's perspective. *Journal of Research Practice, 4*(2), M3. http://jrp.icaap.org/index.php/jrp/article/view/136/154

Rochmyaningsih, D. (March 9, 2012). Indonesia makes research publication a graduation requirement for all students. *Asian Scientist*. http://www.asianscientist.com/2012/03/academia/indonesia-dikti-aptisi-publication-a-graduation-requirement-for-all-students-2012/

Ruano-Borbalan, J.-C. (2022). Doctoral education from its medieval foundations to today's globalisation and standardisation. *European Journal of Education, 57*, 367–380. https://doi.org/10.1111/ejed.12522

Simpson, S. (2013). Systems of writing response: A Brazilian student's experiences writing for publication in an environmental sciences doctoral program. *Research in the Teaching of English, 48*, 228–249.

Sinclair, J., Barnacle, R., & Cuthbert, D. (2014). How the doctorate contributes to the formation of active researchers: What the research tells us. *Studies in Higher Education, 39*, 1972–1986. https://doi.org/10.1080/03075079.2013.806460

Starke-Meyerring, D. (2011). The paradox of writing in doctoral education: Student experiences. In L. McAlpine & C. Amundsen (Eds.), *Doctoral education: Research-based strategies for doctoral students, supervisors and administrators* (pp. 75–95). Springer.

Strauss, P., Walton, J. A., & Madsen, S. (2003). "I don't have time to be an English teacher": Supervising the EAL thesis. *Hong Kong Journal of Applied Linguistics, 8*, 1–16.

Watts, J. H. (2012). To publish or not to publish before submission? Considerations for doctoral students and supervisors. *Creative Education, 3*, 1101–1107. https://doi.org/10.4236/ce.2012.326165

Weidman, J., & Stein, E. (2003). Socialization of doctoral students to academic norms. *Research in Higher Education, 44*, 641–656. https://doi.org/10.1023/a:1026123508335

Williamson, I. O., & Cable, D. M. (2003). Predicting early career research productivity: The case of management faculty. *Journal of Organizational Behavior, 24*, 25–44. https://doi.org/10.1002/job.178

Yamagata-Lynch, L. C. (2007). Confronting analytical dilemmas for understanding complex human interactions in design-based research from a cultural-historical activity theory (CHAT) framework. *Journal of the Learning Sciences, 16*, 451–484. https://doi.org/10.1080/10508400701524777

Yamagata-Lynch, L. C. (2010). *Activity systems analysis methods: Understanding complex learning environments*. Springer.

Yin, R. K. (2009). *Case study research: Design and methods* (4th ed.). Sage.

Chapter 2
Doctoral Publication as a Sociopolitical Practice

This chapter presents the theoretical frameworks that have informed this study. It first outlines the overarching theoretical framework of this research—the social constructivist view of literacy and writing—that has been widely adopted as the theoretical underpinning of research on scholarly publishing. It then takes a critical look at several social constructivist concepts that studies on EAL researchers' scholarly publishing practices have frequently drawn on, including community of practice, discourse community, and legitimate peripheral participation, among others. Following that, it introduces neoliberalism and activity theory, respectively, which serve as the theoretical frameworks for interpreting the findings related to policies, practices and identities surrounding doctoral publication. Finally, this chapter concludes with a summary of the potentials of these theoretical frameworks for addressing some of the substantive and theoretical issues in the extant research.

2.1 Social Constructivist Perspectives on Doctoral Publication

Social constructivist perspectives posit that knowledge production and dissemination are socially, politically, and ideologically situated (McKinley, 2015; Vygotsky, 1978). As such, "writing for scholarly publication is considered as a social practice that is shaped and informed by surrounding socio-contextual discourses and practices and ideological and political forces" (Flowerdew & Habibie, 2022, p. 6; see also Mu, 2020). This view of scholarly publishing can be seen as a synthesis of what Ivanič (2004) identifies as the social practice view of writing and the sociopolitical view of writing.

As a widely adopted theoretical tenet underpinning research on (scholarly) writing, the social practice view of writing underlines "the broader sociocultural context of writing: the social meanings and values of writing, and issues of power"

(Ivanič, 2004, p. 234). In the same vein, the sociopolitical view of writing also foregrounds the context, "but focuses on the broader, more political aspects of context" (Ivanič, 2004, p. 237). Unlike other views on writing (e.g., the creativity, genre, process, and skills perspectives) in the literature (see Ivanič, 1998, 2004; Lillis & Scott, 2007), these two views attach great importance to the roles of context, power, and ideological and political forces in producing text. Thus, a sociopolitical practice view on scholarly publishing focuses more on practice than on text and pays close attention to sociopolitical contexts within which scholarly publishing takes place (see Aitchison et al., 2010; Aitchison & Lee, 2006; Casanave, 2003; Flowerdew & Li, 2009b; Li, 2006a; Lillis & Scott, 2007; Paltridge, 2004; Tardy, 2006; Uzuner, 2008).

There is evidence indicating that power differentials between scholarly writers, especially EAL researchers from the periphery and doctoral students on the one hand, and such gatekeepers as journal editors and reviewers, and supervisors on the other, play an important role in scholarly publishing (Belcher, 2007; Berkenkotter & Huckin, 1995; Cho, 2004; Gosden, 1996; Li, 2006a; Lillis & Scott, 2007). Similarly, research has also shown that navigating power differentials between doctoral students and their supervisors is crucial for successful writing outcomes (Belcher, 1994; Dong, 1996; Hasrati, 2013; Huang, 2010; Lee & Roth, 2003; Li, 2006a; Watson, 2012). In a case study of the coauthoring activity between a doctoral student from Algeria and his main professor, Blakeslee (1997) documented how the power differentials played themselves out as the professor finally appropriated the manuscript produced by the student after several attempts at providing feedback that was implicit to the student and thus not responded to.

As a result of this and other factors (e.g., conventions, rules, and practices of writing), "writers are not entirely free to choose how to represent the world, how to represent themselves, what social role to take, and how to address their readers when they write" (Ivanič, 2004, p. 238). Meanwhile, however, writer agency also has a role to play in this view of writing in that writers can take critical stances towards the status quo by resisting and contesting it and thereby bring about changes to existing practices and power relations. In parallel to these two orientations, Lillis and Scott (2007; see also Hanauer & Englander, 2013) distinguish two approaches to academic literacies: the normative or pragmatic approach and the transformative or critical approach. While the former is interested in identifying conventions and practices and inducting novices or students into them, the latter sees conventions and practices as contestable and meaning making as a site of struggle, and acknowledges and embraces the value of alternative practices and different ways of meaning making.

Research on scholarly publishing has drawn upon both approaches, with some studies focusing more on identifying practices and conventions (e.g., Cheung, 2010; Flowerdew, 1999a, 1999b, 2008; Lillis & Curry, 2006a), and others more on critiquing and contesting them (e.g., Canagarajah, 2002a, 2002b; Casanave, 2008; Gosden, 2003; Lillis & Curry, 2006b). These two orientations, however, are not to be seen as dichotomous but complementary, a position that has been characterised as critical pragmatism in the literature (see Benesch, 2001; Flowerdew, 2007; Hanauer & Englander, 2013; Harwood & Hadley, 2004). On the one hand, we may

2.1 Social Constructivist Perspectives on Doctoral Publication

run the risk of blindly reproducing unequal conventions and practices if we only take a normative approach. On the other, a transformative approach alone may do a disservice to EAL researchers and doctoral students because apprenticing EAL researchers and doctoral students into dominant conventions and practices can be an empowering approach, an approach that may be endorsed by many EAL researchers and doctoral students (Flowerdew, 2007; Tang, 2012). Therefore, studies that draw on both orientations hold valuable implications for EAL and novice researchers' scholarly publishing endeavours. The normative approach may be more useful and appropriate for novices, though they may need or want to take the transformative approach as they become increasingly fuller members of the community (see, e.g., Kubota, 2003, for her autobiographical account of this changing need).

Whichever approach is taken, scholarly publishing as a sociopolitical practice is imbued with power work, such as negotiation with powerful gatekeepers (e.g., Belcher, 2007; Blakeslee, 1997), appropriation or transformation of writer identities (e.g., Englander, 2009; Shi, 2003), and negotiation of textual norms and conventions (e.g., Canagarajah, 2002a; Shi, 2003), to name just a few. The role of power in scholarly publishing, as noted above, may be particularly salient for EAL researchers and doctoral students who tend to have limited power, status, and/or access in their attempts to participate in the scholarly publishing activity. Couched within the sociopolitical practice view of scholarly publishing, previous research has drawn upon several sociopolitical concepts to explore and unpack EAL and novice researchers' motives, challenges, and strategies for scholarly publishing. These concepts include Kachru's (1986) concentric circles, the World Systems proposed by Galtung (1971, 1980) and Wallerstein (1991), and several notions related to situated learning theories—community of practice (CoP), discourse community (DC), and legitimate periphery participation (LPP) (Brown et al., 1989; Lave & Wenger, 1991; Rogoff, 1995; Wenger, 1998).

From a social constructivist perspective, EAL researchers' scholarly publishing is mediated by geolinguistics and geopolitics—issues of unequal power, status, and access related to different languages and geographical locations in scholarly publishing (Canagarajah, 2002a; Flowerdew, 2000; Lillis & Curry, 2010; Liu, 2004). Two sets of concepts—Kachru's (1986) concentric circles and the World Systems (Galtung, 1971, 1980; Wallerstein, 1991)—have been widely used to describe and explain those issues (see Canagarajah, 2002a; Lillis & Curry, 2010). Kachru's concentric framework, mainly concerned with the use and status of English, consists of three circles of countries and regions. The Inner Circle refers to the five native English-speaking countries (i.e., Australia, Canada, New Zealand, the UK, and the US); the Outer Circle represents former colonies that use English as a second or official language (e.g., India, Nigeria, Singapore), and the Expanding Circle comprises countries that use English as a foreign language (e.g., Japan, Korea, Chinese mainland). There exist power differentials between the Inner Circle, on the one hand, and the Outer and Expanding Circles, on the other, which roughly correspond to the Centre and the Periphery in the World Systems (e.g., Galtung, 1971, 1980; Wallerstein, 1991; see also Curry & Lillis, 2004; Lillis & Curry, 2010).

Specifically, inequalities in power, status, and access between the Centre and the Periphery play themselves out in EAL researchers' choice of languages for publication and give rise to conflicts and tensions that they have to negotiate in their attempts at publishing and learning to publish. Although both sets of concepts have been proven useful in illuminating issues of power, status, and access involved in EAL researchers' scholarly publishing, they pay insufficient attention to the local social, cultural, and institutional contexts within which scholarly publishing takes place, and tend to downplay or neglect heterogeneity within each context (Lillis & Curry, 2010).

The concept of network (Curry & Lillis, 2010; Lillis & Curry, 2006b, 2010) seems to have more descriptive and explanatory power than such notions as the Inner Circle, the Outer Circle, the Expanding Circle, the Centre, and the Periphery. This concept posits scholarly publishing activity as networked activity, and competence in scholarly publishing as networked rather than individual competence (Curry & Lillis, 2010; Lillis & Curry, 2006b, 2010). However, despite its advantages, this concept also has several limitations. First, it focuses largely on people who are important in building and retaining networks and neglects others who, though not crucial in networking, play important roles in EAL researchers' scholarly publishing activities (e.g., language editors). Second, research (e.g., Casanave & Vandrick, 2003; Flowerdew & Li, 2007) has shown that EAL researchers may rely on published journal articles or other cultural artefacts for "textual mentorship" in their scholarly writing and publishing. These and other factors are not accorded due attention in the network framework. As will be illustrated below, however, these factors play vital roles in EAL researchers' scholarly publishing activities.

Under the influence of social constructivism, the bulk of previous research on learning to write for publication has employed situated learning theories to understand and explain novice researchers' apprenticeship in scholarly publishing (see Flowerdew & Li, 2009; Hyland, 2009; Uzuner, 2008). From a situated learning perspective, learning can be broadly defined as a process whereby less experienced people actively participate in a socioculturally organised activity with the help of more experienced people and/or cultural artefacts (e.g., language, texts) to develop mastery of the activity and to obtain fuller membership of a given community of practice (CoP), within which the activity is situated (Brown et al., 1989; Lave & Wenger, 1991; Rogoff, 1995; Wenger, 1998). Viewed this way, situated learning theories mesh well with the sociopolitical practice view of writing discussed above, which sees scholarly publishing as a sociopolitically situated activity fraught with negotiation of power, status, and access.

Two sets of notions in situated learning theories have been frequently used to unpack EAL and novice researchers' learning to write for publication, namely, community of practice (CoP) or discourse community (DC) (e.g., Flowerdew, 2000; Li, 2006b) and legitimate peripheral participation (LPP) (e.g., Canagarajah, 2003; Casanave, 1998; Cho, 2004; Flowerdew, 2000; Li, 2005, 2006a, 2007; Shi, 2003). While CoP and/or DC are often drawn on to "describe the inner workings of core academic communities and multilingual scholars' position in these social settings," the notion of LPP is typically adopted to explicate the main mechanism of learning for

2.1 Social Constructivist Perspectives on Doctoral Publication

novice researchers (Uzuner, 2008, p. 258). Similarly, in their discussion of academic enculturation, Prior and Bilbro (2012) also note that while DCs, CoPs and other similar concepts are often employed to conceptualise the space of learning, LPP and similar concepts are often used to theorise the content and mechanism of learning. In what follows, I briefly discuss and critique these concepts and issues related to them.

Community of Practice (CoP) and Discourse Community (DC)

Swales (1990) identifies "six defining characteristics" (p. 24) of a DC: (1) common goals, (2) communication mechanisms, (3) participatory mechanisms, (4) specific genres, (5) specific lexis, and (6) a high level of content and discoursal expertise. Likewise, Wenger (1998) proposes three essential characteristics of a CoP: (1) mutual engagement, (2) a joint enterprise, and (3) a shared repertoire. Their respective defining characteristics suggest that DC emphasises texts or genres oriented towards some shared purpose (Johns, 1997; Swales, 1990; Woodward-Kron, 2004), whereas CoP highlights practice or activity that holds the community together, as "practice is the source of coherence of a community" (Wenger, 1998, p. 72). Despite their varying foci, both concepts provide useful ways to discuss the securing and maintaining of the membership of a DC or CoP and the factors involved in the process (see Berkenkotter & Huckin, 1995; Flowerdew, 2000; Myers, 1985). In particular, they offer a language for describing and explicating interactions among people who are engaged in either language/discourse or activity/practice geared towards some joint purpose. Meanwhile, they also provide a vocabulary for discussing issues of power, status, and access in relation to membership, particularly between novices and experts of a DC or CoP (Liu, 2004; Prior, 1998). Further, Curry and Lillis (2004) argue that these concepts, along with the concept of speech community, can also be used "to explore the relationships between text and practice, that is, how people learn the rules governing both texts and practices and thus participate in maintaining and developing them" (p. 665) and to discuss "who scholars are writing to and for, and why" (p. 666).

Useful as they are, there is much controversy over what exactly CoP and DC refer to and their internal workings (Bizzell, 1992; Ivanič, 1998; Prior, 1998, 2003). Hence, they are considered to be "invaluable but problematic" (Hyland & Hamp-Lyons, 2002, p. 7). Conceptualised as bounded groups, DCs and CoPs may give the impression of being homogeneous and static. In this regard, Hyland and Hamp-Lyons (2002) warn against "framing discourse communities as determinate, static, autonomous, and predictable arenas of shared and agreed upon values and conventions" (p. 7). In contrast to this "homogeneous and static" view, however, there is a growing recognition that both DCs and CoPs are heterogeneous and dynamic (Barton & Tusting, 2005; Casanave, 1995; Prior, 1998; Starfield, 2007; Swales, 2004). First, DCs and CoPs may have sub-communities, and boundaries between communities tend to be diffuse. Therefore, individuals may belong to multiple DCs or CoPs at the same time. Further, as Hyland and Hamp-Lyons (2002) point out, "it has not been easy to agree on exactly what the term [DC] means" (p. 7), and DCs have been used to refer to disciplines, university departments, users of an internet list, 'invisible colleges,' among many others. Similarly, although Wenger proposes four components of a CoP in his 1998 book, these components themselves—meaning, practice, community, and identity—are too broad and abstract to be useful for integrated analyses involving all of them (see Edwards, 2005; Storberg-Walker, 2008). On the one hand, this elusive nature of DCs and CoPs points to their dynamic nature; on the other, it makes it difficult to pin down parties or factors involved in a DC or CoP. In regard to this, Hyland and Hamp-Lyons (2002) caution against "reducing communities to aggregates of competing and indeterminate voices" (p. 7).

Thus, it seems that DCs and CoPs are characterised by both stability and change, which are enacted in part by the continuous processes of accepting newcomers and displacing old-timers (Lave & Wenger, 1991; Wenger, 1998). In particular, the acceptance or apprenticeship of newcomers into DCs or CoPs has been a subject of much discussion and research. As regards writing for publication, apprenticeship of newcomers is often characterised as (discourse/language) socialisation (Duff, 2010; Garrett & Baquedano-López, 2002), academic enculturation (Prior & Bilbro, 2012), or LPP (Flowerdew & Li, 2009; Uzuner, 2008). As most studies on writing for publication have used LPP as an exploratory concept, I discuss only LPP here (but see Duff, 2010; Garrett & Baquedano-López, 2002; Prior & Bilbro, 2012 for reviews of the other two concepts).

Legitimate Peripheral Participation (LPP)

In line with the definition of learning endorsed by situated learning theories, LPP is a process of 'learning through apprenticeship'—a process of moving towards full participation in the practice of a CoP and towards full membership in the CoP (Lave & Wenger, 1991; Wenger, 1998). As an analytical lens for the mechanism of learning, LPP has several undergirding tenets that distinguish itself from other theories of learning and make it a useful perspective on learning to write for publication. First, in contrast to traditional theories that see learning as occurring through formal instruction,[1] LPP foregrounds the role of 'participation' in learning, as evidenced in its conceptualisation of learning as "an integral aspect of practice (in a historical, generative sense)" (Lave & Wenger, 1991, pp. 34–35) and "not something we do when we do nothing else or stop doing when we do something else" (Wenger, 1998, p. 8). This is cogently captured by Brown et al. (1989):

> Given the chance to observe and practice *in situ* the behavior of members of a culture, people pick up relevant jargon, imitate behavior, and gradually start to act in accordance with its norms. These cultural practices are often recondite and extremely complex. Nonetheless, given the opportunity to observe and practice them, people adopt them with great success. (p. 34)

Furthermore, LPP postulates that participation is 'legitimate' yet 'peripheral.' The notion of 'legitimate' refers to "a defining characteristic of ways of belonging" (Lave & Wenger, 1991, p. 35). Therefore, whether or to what extent novices are treated as potential members of a CoP is crucial to their participation in the CoP

---

[1] It should be noted that while foregrounding the importance of practice for learning, LPP does not deny the usefulness of formal instruction for learning (Lave & Wenger, 1991).

2.1 Social Constructivist Perspectives on Doctoral Publication

and hence their learning because "[o]nly with legitimacy can all their inevitable stumblings and violations become opportunities for learning rather than cause for dismissal, neglect, or exclusion" (Lave & Wenger, 1991, p. 101). Peripherality means "multiple, varied, more- or less-engaged and—inclusive ways of being located in the fields of participation defined by a community" (Lave & Wenger, 1991, p. 36). In this sense, peripherality does not have the negative connotation normally associated with it. Indeed, legitimate peripherality is seen as "a place in which one moves toward more-intensive participation" (Lave & Wenger, 1991, p. 36).

Despite these positive connotations, LPP or learning is not necessarily a smooth process, given that unequal power relations are ubiquitous in CoPs. Lave and Wenger (1991), for example, observe that "[h]egemony over resources for learning and alienation from full participation are inherent in the shaping of the legitimacy and peripherality of participation in its historical realizations" (p. 42). Therefore, old-timers or gate-keepers of a CoP and the CoP as a whole play a pivotal role in newcomers' 'inbound trajectories' by granting or denying them legitimacy to access learning resources and opportunities. Similarly, newcomers may face difficulties in claiming expertise due to power imbalance between themselves and experts, despite the growing recognition that expertise or mastery "resides not in the master but in the organization of the community of practice of which the master is a part" (Lave & Wenger, 1991, p. 94) and is thus contestable (e.g., Brown et al., 1989; Duff, 2007; Morita & Kobayashi, 2008).

Second, LPP entails not only the acquisition of the knowledge and skills involved in the practice of a CoP or of the beliefs, values, and ideologies underlying it, but it also "implies becoming a different person" (Lave & Wenger, 1991, p. 53). In this sense, learning and becoming are inseparable and are the two sides of the same coin. Therefore, "[m]oving toward full participation in practice involves not just a greater commitment of time, intensified effort, more and broader responsibilities within the community, and more difficult and risky tasks, but, more importantly, an increasing sense of identity as a master practitioner" (Lave & Wenger, 1991, p. 111). Further, as discussed above, the norms and conventions of a DC or a CoP also undergo changes with newcomers joining the DC or CoP and bringing along new perspectives and practices. In this regard, Lave and Wenger (1991) maintain that "change is a fundamental property of communities of practice and their activities" (p. 117). Therefore, the individual and the community are mutually reproduced and transformed.

It is evident that LPP is a useful conceptual lens, through which (informal) learning can be richly understood and theorised. However, because it focuses on the novice-master movement—i.e., the vertical dimension of learning, it tends to fall short of describing and theorising the horizontal dimension of learning characterised by "moving from one community of practice to another" (Wenger, 1998, p. 103; see also Akkerman & Bakker, 2011; Engeström et al., 1995). Researchers are often engaged with multiple communities and in diverse and sometimes competing activities at the same time. As a result, their scholarly publishing practices inevitably involve both vertical and horizontal movements. Therefore, a theoretical framework that can capture both vertical and horizontal movements may shed more light on EAL novice researchers' scholarly publishing practices.

In summary, although the theoretical concepts reviewed above—the Inner, Outer, and Expanding Circles, the Centre and the Periphery, and CoPs, DCs, networks, and LPP—have contributed greatly to our understanding of EAL and novice researchers' scholarly publishing practices, they have several limitations that might have precluded more in-depth explorations of some issues (Flowerdew & Habibie, 2022). First, because Kachru's concentric circles and the concepts of Centre and Periphery in the World Systems focus predominantly on geolinguistic and geopolitical contexts and since the CoP and DC notions are somewhat elusive, these concepts tend to fall short of capturing how broader (e.g., globalisation and marketisation of higher education) as well as more local and specific social, cultural, and institutional contexts (e.g., the context of doctoral study) may shape researchers' scholarly publishing practices and evolving identities. Second, while capable of capturing local and special sociocultural contexts, network as a concept tends to gloss over the role of cultural artefacts in researchers' scholarly publishing practices. Third, because LPP focuses on movements from novices to experts in a DC or CoP, it is not well equipped to describe and explain researchers' movement between different activities, which is becoming increasingly common in today's complex world. There is thus a need for more situated and versatile theoretical frameworks to shed new light on EAL doctoral students' scholarly publishing practices. As I will explicate below, neoliberalism and activity theory constitute suitable theoretical frameworks to redress some of the aforementioned concerns.

2.2 Neoliberal Perspectives on Doctoral Publication

Neoliberalism refers to an economic and political theory that tends to favour competition, free trade, privatisation of state assets, and deregulation of markets (Harvey, 2005) and embrace "a governing social and political rationality that submits all human activities, values, institutions, and practices to market principles" (Brown, 2011, p. 118). Several tenets underlying neoliberalism are closely related to doctoral publication, including marketisation, managerial accountability, and auditing culture (Lynch, 2015; Olssen & Peters, 2005; Schmeichel et al., 2017; Smyth, 2017).

Neoliberalism has accelerated the marketisation of higher education in general and research publication in particular over the past few decades (Giroux, 2002; Lillis & Curry, 2010). Under the influence of marketisation, research publication is conceptualised "as a measurable commodity" (Curry & Lillis, 2018, p. 3) and is increasingly linked to promotion, merit pay, and/or monetary rewards (Giroux, 2003; Harris, 2005; Lillis, 2012). As a result, institutions and individual researchers are increasingly rewarded or punished based on "the number of articles published, the national or international scope of the publications, and the indexing of those journals in a database" (Hanauer & Englander, 2013, p. 8). These rewards systems privilege the exchange value over the use value of research publication and often

2.2 Neoliberal Perspectives on Doctoral Publication

assign varying (exchange) value to "different kinds of scholarly publishing (text type, specific category of journal, etc.)", creating stratifications among different kinds of research (Lillis, 2012, p. 702; see also Curry & Lillis, 2018; Feng et al., 2013; Lee & Lee, 2013). It is thus little wonder that research outputs published in internationally-indexed (e.g., Science Citation Index [SCI]) English-medium journals tend to be more valorised than their counterparts in local non-English-medium journals.

Consequently, researchers may "have little option but to publish in English and on issues construed as significant to an English-speaking world", as aptly captured in the mantra of "you either publish in English or you perish" (Hanauer & Englander, 2013, p. 11). The same is true for doctoral publication, as evinced by the mantra of 'publish SCI papers or no degree' (Li, 2016). However, the premium placed on the exchange value of international English-medium publications is likely to compromise the "immediate 'use value'" of local publications (Lillis, 2012, p. 715) and sabotage local scholarship and research cultures (Feng et al., 2013; Mu & Zhang, 2018; Salager-Meyer, 2008). Moreover, the privileging of the exchange value of research publication may prompt multilingual researchers, including doctoral students, to give up their "commitment to, and interests in, publishing in local languages for local audiences" for the greater exchange value of publishing in international English-medium journals (Curry & Lillis, 2018, p. 2; see also Casanave, 1998; Li & Flowerdew, 2009). In the long run, the marketisation of research publication is inclined to undermine researchers' autonomy in choosing what to research and where to publish their research (Curry & Lillis, 2018; Feng et al., 2013; Gao & Zheng, 2020; Lillis, 2012).

Closely related to marketisation is market-driven managerial accountability, another important tenet of neoliberalism. Managerial accountability emphasises "the achievement of pre-set targets and externally imposed objectives" (Olssen & Peters, 2005, p. 328; see also Schmeichel et al., 2017). In contrast to managerial accountability, professional accountability prioritises professional standards and internal objectives (Olssen & Peters, 2005; Schmeichel et al., 2017). Despite their contradictory standards and objectives, both managerial and professional accountability may have a role to play in managing and accounting for research publication. In a study of supervisor roles in Chinese doctoral students' scholarly publishing efforts, for example, the supervisors were found to play not only managerial roles ('prey searchers' and managers of students' publishing endeavours) but also professional roles (e.g., manuscript correctors and 'masters') (Lei & Hu, 2015). However, managerial accountability tends to compel researcher to respond to "targets, indicators and evaluations" (Ball, 2003, p. 215) and hold them accountable for their performances (Curry & Lillis, 2018; Gao & Zheng, 2020). As a result, it is likely to prevail over professional accountability in research publication, which may in turn compromise researchers' professional beliefs and values, and erode their autonomy and agency in scholarly publication (Deem, 2004; Gao & Zheng, 2020; Harris, 2005; Sandy & Shen, 2019).

Another central tenet underlying neoliberalism that has shaped and reshaped scholarly publication is the auditing culture. The auditing culture is characterised by regular checking and monitoring of institutions' and researchers' measurable research outputs (Lynch, 2015; Olssen & Peters, 2005). Regular checking, evaluating, and auditing of institutions' performances are believed to enhance their productivity and competitiveness (Gao & Zheng, 2020; Suspitsyna, 2010). In a similar vein, institutions have in turn increasingly adopted the auditing culture and started to monitor, assess, and audit researchers' performances and productivity (Curry & Lillis, 2018; Englander & Uzuner-Smith, 2013; Lee & Lee, 2013; Li & Yang, 2018). In order to boost research productivity, the auditing culture encourages measurable research outputs to the detriment of knowledge production (Ball, 2003, 2012; Harris, 2005; Sandy & Shen, 2019). Consequently, "[t]he traditional professional culture of open intellectual enquiry and debate has been replaced with an institutional stress on performativity, as evidenced by the emergence of an emphasis on measured outputs" (Olssen & Peters, 2005, p. 313). As observed by Ball (2012, p. 19), in the auditing culture, "experience is nothing, productivity is everything". To 'game' the research assessment system, for instance, researchers are likely to choose safe, short-term research topics over risky, long-term research projects (O'Regan & Gray, 2018). Moreover, because it endorses competition, rating, and ranking, the auditing culture may impair "professional judgement and co-operation" (Ball, 2003, p. 218).

These influences of neoliberalism have impinged not only on researchers but also on doctoral students, as evidenced by the increasing institutionalisation of doctoral publication as a graduation requirement. Doctoral students are consequently under mounting pressure to get published while juggling multiple activities during their doctoral studies. In view of the power-ridden nature of scholarly publishing and doctoral students' juggling between multiple activities, activity theory provides a useful framework for exploring doctoral publication.

2.3 Activity Theory Perspectives on Doctoral Publication

Kuutti (1996) defines activity theory as "a philosophical and cross-disciplinary framework for studying different kinds of human practices as developmental processes, with both individual and social levels interlinked at the same time" (p. 25). It originated from several strands of thoughts, namely, Marx's historical dialectical materialism, the German philosophy from Kant to Hegel, and Russian cultural psychology (Engeström, 1999; Roth & Lee, 2007). These thoughts converge on the effort to bridge the dualism of mind and world, positing that human consciousness is inseparable from its material conditions and is dialectically related to the world. The overcoming of the dualism opened up possibilities for a new set of sociocultural theories of learning that differ fundamentally from earlier behaviourist and cognitivist models of learning in their varying emphasis on the social, cultural, and historical context. As a sociocultural theory of learning and development, activity theory places an emphasis on social and cultural contexts, and shares their theoretical origin in Vygotsky's conceptualisation of human action and cognition as being mediated by cultural artefacts (Artemeva, 2008; Barab et al., 2004; Engeström & Miettinen, 1999; Tardy, 2006). As the unit of analysis in activity theory, activity system or network of activity systems is well specified and equipped to examine the local social, cultural, and institutional contexts of doctoral students' scholarly publishing activities. In addition, with its analytical concepts such as boundary object, boundary crossing and contradiction, activity theory is capable of capturing the interactions and potential disjunctures between doctoral students' scholarly publishing activity system and other activity systems.

Activity theory has evolved through three generations (see Engeström, 2001; Engeström & Miettinen, 1999; Roth & Lee, 2007). Built on Vygotsky's idea of mediation, first-generation activity theory established some of the most important tenets undergirding the theory, including the concept of cultural mediation, the notion of the zone of proximal development (ZPD), and the dialectical relationship between subject and object. Vygotsky's (1978, 1981) idea of mediation postulates that human cognition is not simply a response to a stimulus but is inherently mediated by material and symbolic tools. This conception of mediation is schematically represented by the well-known triangle of stimulus, response, and a mediating artefact (a tool or sign). Thus, the notion of mediation points to the mediated nature of human action and cognition, thereby bridging the Cartesian split of mind and world or subject and object.

Drawing mainly on Leont'ev's work (1978/2009, 1981), second-generation activity theory shifts the unit of analysis from individual action to collective activity by specifying the hierarchical levels of an activity system, an important contribution made by Leont'ev to activity theory (Barab et al., 2004; DeVane & Squire, 2012; Engeström, 1987, 2001; Kozulin, 1986; Roth, 2007; Witte & Haas, 2005). In his classical example of the primeval collective hunt, Lenot'ev (1978/2009) introduced the notion of division of labour (e.g., beating the bush and slaying the game) and a related notion, object-oriented, collective activity system. He noted that the individual action of 'beating the bush' can only be meaningfully understood when considered in light of the collective activity system or the object of hunting the animal for food or clothes. This hierarchy of activity system helps to overcome the tautology of explaining the phenomenon of individual action with the concept of individual action. As a consequence, motive-driven, object-oriented, and collective activity systems become the explanatory principle, whereas goal-directed actions and condition-based operations become the objects (subject matters) of study. Therefore, activity theory can serve as both a theoretical framework and an analytical tool (Barab et al., 2002).

Despite being a well-developed theoretical framework, second-generation activity theory focuses on single activity systems and cannot capture modern human activity featuring simultaneous and continuous engagement in multiple activity systems, or what Engeström et al. (1995) refer to as polycontextuality. The third-generation activity theory expands on second-generation activity theory and extends the unit of analysis to a network of interacting activity systems in order to "understand dialogue, multiple perspectives, and networks of interacting activity systems" (Engeström, 2001, p. 135; see also Engeström & Miettinen, 1999; Russell & Yañez, 2003). With at least two interacting activity systems, this generation of activity theory is particularly useful in understanding horizontal learning or simultaneous engagement in increasingly complex and interrelated activity systems (Akkerman & Bakker, 2011;

Daniels, 2008; Engeström, 2001, 2010; Tuomi-Gröhn & Engeström, 2007; Tuomi-Gröhn et al., 2007). In contrast to vertical learning characteristic of the novice-expert transformation, horizontal learning as conceptualised in activity theory is characterised by "mov[ing] between multiple parallel activity contexts" and "negotiating and combining ingredients from different contexts to achieve hybrid solutions" (Engeström et al., 1995, p. 319).

To conclude this section, activity theory takes activity system or network of activity systems as its unit of analysis (Barab et al., 2004; Engeström & Miettinen, 1999) and is thus well equipped to capture possible connections and interactions between activities and potential challenges in making the connections and interactions. As doctoral students tend to engage in multiple activities while attempting to publish, activity theory provides a promising theoretical framework to unpack their publishing practices and evolving identities.

2.4 Conclusion

This chapter has outlined the sociopolitical practice view of writing widely adopted as the theoretical underpinning of research on scholarly publishing. It has also reviewed and critiqued several sociopolitical concepts frequently used in the literature to explore EAL researchers' scholarly publishing practices. In reviewing and critiquing these concepts, it has revealed that some of the theoretical concepts adopted in previous research focused on broad sociopolitical contexts and tended to gloss over local and specific contexts within which scholarly publishing activities take place (e.g., the context of doctoral study for doctoral publication). Additionally, it has also shown the limited potential of situated learning theories to address doctoral students' simultaneous engagement in multiple activity systems. In response, it has advanced neoliberalism and activity theory as theoretical frameworks that are capable of bridging the gaps between the broad and the local contexts for doctoral publication, and unveiling the connections between policies, practices, and identities related to doctoral publication.

References

Aitchison, C., Kamler, B., & Lee, A. (2010). Introduction: Why publishing pedagogies? In C. Aitchison, B. Kamler, & A. Lee (Eds.), *Publishing pedagogies for the doctorate and beyond* (pp. 1–11). Routledge.

Aitchison, C., & Lee, A. (2006). Research writing: Problems and pedagogies. *Teaching in Higher Education, 11*, 265–278. https://doi.org/10.1080/13562510600680574

Akkerman, S. F., & Bakker, A. (2011). Boundary crossing and boundary objects. *Review of Educational Research, 81*, 132–169. https://doi.org/10.3102/0034654311404435

Artemeva, N. (2008). Toward a unified social theory of genre learning. *Journal of Business and Technical Communication, 22*, 160–185. https://doi.org/10.1177/1050651907311925

References

Ball, S. J. (2003). The teacher's soul and the terrors of performativity. *Journal of Education Policy, 18*, 215–228. https://doi.org/10.1080/0268093022000043065

Ball, S. J. (2012). Performativity, commodification and commitment: An I-spy guide to the neoliberal university. *British Journal of Educational Studies, 60*, 17–28. https://doi.org/10.1080/00071005.2011.650940

Barab, S. A., Barnett, M. l., Yamagata-Lynch, L. C., Squire, K., & Keating, T. (2002). Using activity theory to understand the systemic tensions characterizing a technology-rich introductory astronomy course. *Mind, Culture, and Activity, 9*, 76–107. https://doi.org/10.1207/s15327884mca0902_02

Barab, S. A., Evans, M. A., & Baek, E. O. (2004). Activity theory as a lens for characterizing the participatory unit. In D. H. Jonassen (Ed.), *Handbook of research on educational communities and technology* (pp. 199–214). Lawrence Erlbaum.

Barton, D., & Tusting, K. (Eds.). (2005). *Beyong communities of practice: Language, power, and social context*. Cambridge University Press.

Belcher, D. (1994). The apprenticeship approach to advanced academic literacy: Graduate students and their mentors. *English for Specific Purposes, 13*, 23–34. https://doi.org/10.1016/0889-4906(94)90022-1

Belcher, D. (2007). Seeking acceptance in an English-only research world. *Journal of Second Language Writing, 16*, 1–22. https://doi.org/10.1016/j.jslw.2006.12.001

Benesch, S. (2001). *Critical English for academic purposes: Theory, politics, pratice*. Lawrence Erlbaum.

Berkenkotter, C., & Huckin, T. N. (1995). *Genre knowledge in disciplinary communication: Cognition/culture/power*. Lawrence Erlbaum.

Bizzell, P. (1992). *Academic discourse and critical consciousness*. University of Pittsburgh Press.

Blakeslee, A. M. (1997). Activity, context, interaction, and authority. *Journal of Business and Technical Communication, 11*, 125–169. https://doi.org/10.1177/1050651997011002001

Brown, J. S., Collins, A., & Duguid, P. (1989). Situated cognition and the culture of learning. *Educational Researcher, 18*, 32–42. https://doi.org/10.3102/0013189x018001032

Brown, W. (2011). Neoliberalized knowledge. *History of the Present, 1*, 113–129.

Canagarajah, A. S. (2002a). *A geopolitics of academic writing*. University of Pittsburgh Press.

Canagarajah, A. S. (2002b). Multilingual writers and the academic community: Towards a critical relationship. *Journal of English for Academic Purposes, 1*, 29–44. https://doi.org/10.1016/s1475-1585(02)00007-3

Canagarajah, A. S. (2003). A somewhat legitimate and very peripheral participation. In C. P. Casanave & S. Vandrick (Eds.), *Writing for scholarly publication: Behind the scenes in language education* (pp. 197–210). Lawrence Erlbaum.

Casanave, C. P., & Vandrick, S. (Eds.). (2003). *Writing for scholarly publication: Behind the scenes in language education*. Lawrence Erlbaum.

Casanave, C. P. (1995). Local interactions: Constructing context for composing in a graduate sociology program. In D. Belcher & G. Graine (Eds.), *Academic writing in a second language: Essays on research and pedagogy* (pp. 83–110). Ablex.

Casanave, C. P. (1998). Transitions: The balancing act of bilingual academics. *Journal of Second Language Writing, 12*, 175–203. https://doi.org/10.1016/S1060-3743(98)90012-1

Casanave, C. P. (2003). Looking ahead to more sociopolitically-oriented case study research in L2 writing scholarship (But should it be called "post-process"?). *Journal of Second Language Writing, 12*, 85–102. https://doi.org/10.1016/s1060-3743(03)00002-x

Casanave, C. P. (2008). The stigmatizing effect of Goffman's stigma label: A response to John Flowerdew. *Journal of English for Academic Purposes, 7*, 264–267. https://doi.org/10.1016/j.jeap.2008.10.013

Cheung, Y. L. (2010). First publications in refereed English journals: Difficulties, coping strategies, and recommendations for student training. *System, 38*, 134–141. https://doi.org/10.1016/j.system.2009.12.012

Cho, S. (2004). Challenges of entering discourse communities through publishing in English: Perspectives of nonnative-speaking doctoral students in the United States of America. *Journal of Language, Identity & Education, 3*, 47–72. https://doi.org/10.1207/s15327701jlie0301_3

Curry, M. J., & Lillis, T. (2004). Multilingual scholars and the imperative to publish in English: Negotiating interests, demands, and rewards. *TESOL Quarterly, 38*, 663–688. https://doi.org/10.2307/3588284

Curry, M. J., & Lillis, T. (2010). Academic research networks: Accessing resources for English-medium publishing. *English for Specific Purposes, 29*, 281–295. https://doi.org/10.1016/j.esp.2010.06.002

Curry, M. J., & Lillis, T. (2018). Problematising English as the privileged language of global academic publishing. In M. J. Curry & T. Lillis (Eds.), *Global academic publishing: Policies, perspectives, and pedagogies* (pp. 1–20). Multilingual Matters.

Daniels, H. (2008). *Vygotsky and research*. Routledge.

Deem, R. (2004). The knowledge worker, the manager-academic and the contemporary UK university: New and old forms of public management? *Financial Accountability & Management, 20*, 107–128. https://doi.org/10.1111/j.1468-0408.2004.00189.x

DeVane, B., & Squire, K. D. (2012). Activity theory in the learning technologies. In D. H. Jonassen & S. Land (Eds.), *Theoretical foundations of learning environments* (2nd ed., pp. 242–267). Routledge.

Dong, Y. R. (1996). Learning how to use citations for knowledge transformation: Non-native doctoral students' dissertation writing in science. *Research in the Teaching of English, 30*, 428–457.

Duff, P. A. (2010). Language socialization into academic discourse communities. *Annual Review of Applied Linguistics, 30*, 169–192. https://doi.org/10.1017/S0267190510000048

Duff, P. A. (2007). Problematising academic discourse socialisation. In H. Marriott, T. Moore, R. Spence-Brown, & R. Melbourne (Eds.), *Learning discourses and the discourses of learning* (pp. 1–18). Monash University e-Press/University of Sydney Press.

Edwards, A. (2005). Let's get beyond community and practice: The many meanings of learning by participating. *The Curriculum Journal, 16*, 49–65. https://doi.org/10.1080/0958517042000336809

Engeström, Y. (1987). *Learning by expanding: An activity-theoretical approach to developmental research*. Orienta-Konsultit.

Engeström, Y. (1999). Activity theory and individual and social transformation. In Y. Engeström, R. Miettinen, & R. Punamäki (Eds.), *Perspectives on activity theory* (pp. 19–38). Cambridge University Press.

Engeström, Y. (2001). Expansive learning at work: Toward an activity theoretical reconceptualization. *Journal of Education and Work, 14*, 133–156.

Engeström, Y. (2010). Activity theory and learning at work. In M. Malloch, L. Cairns, K. Evans, & B. N. O'Connor (Eds.), *The Sage handbook of workplace learning* (pp. 74–89). Sage.

Engeström, Y., Engeström, R., & Kärkkäinen, M. (1995). Polycontextuality and boundary crossing in expert cognition: Learning and problem solving in complex work activities. *Learning and Instruction, 5*, 319–336. https://doi.org/10.1016/0959-4752(95)00021-6

Engeström, Y., & Miettinen, R. (1999). Introduction. In Y. Engeström, R. Miettinen, & R. Punamäki (Eds.), *Perspectives on activity theory* (pp. 1–16). Cambridge University Press.

Englander, K. (2009). Transformation of the identities of nonnative English-speaking scientists as a consequence of the social construction of revision. *Journal of Language, Identity & Education, 8*, 35–53. https://doi.org/10.1080/15348450802619979

Englander, K., & Uzuner-Smith, S. (2013). The role of policy in constructing the peripheral scientist in the era of globalization. *Language Policy, 12*, 231–250. https://doi.org/10.1007/s10993-012-9268-1

Feng, H., Beckett, G., & Huang, D. (2013). From 'import' to 'import—export' oriented internationalization: The impact of national policy on scholarly publication in China. *Language Policy, 12*, 251–272. https://doi.org/10.1007/s10993-013-9285-8

References

Flowerdew, J. (1999a). Problems in writing for scholarly publication in English: The case of Hong Kong. *Journal of Second Language Writing, 8*, 243–264. https://doi.org/10.1016/s1060-3743(99)80116-7

Flowerdew, J. (1999b). Writing for scholarly publication in English: The case of Hong Kong. *Journal of Second Language Writing, 8*, 123–145. https://doi.org/10.1016/s1060-3743(99)80125-8

Flowerdew, J. (2000). Discourse community, legitimate peripheral participation, and the nonnative-English-speaking scholar. *TESOL Quarterly, 34*, 127–150. https://doi.org/10.2307/3588099

Flowerdew, J. (2007). The non-Anglophone scholar on the periphery of scholarly publication. *AILA Review, 20*, 14–27. https://doi.org/10.1075/aila.20.04flo

Flowerdew, J. (2008). Scholarly writers who use English as an additional language: What can Goffman's "Stigma" tell us? *Journal of English for Academic Purposes, 7*, 77–86. https://doi.org/10.1016/j.jeap.2008.03.002

Flowerdew, J., & Habibie, P. (2022). *Introducing English for research publication purposes*. Routledge.

Flowerdew, J., & Li, Y. (2007). Language re-use among Chinese apprentice scientists writing for publication. *Applied Linguistics, 28*, 440–465. https://doi.org/10.1093/applin/amm031

Flowerdew, J., & Li, Y. (2009). The globalisation of scholarship: Studying Chinese scholars writing for international publication. In R. M. Manchón (Ed.), *Writing in foreign language contexts: Learning, teaching, and research* (pp. 156–182). Multilingual Matters.

Galtung, J. (1980). *The true worlds: A transnational perspective*. Free Press.

Galtung, J. (1971). A structural theory of imperialism. *Journal of Peace Research, 8*, 81–117. https://doi.org/10.1177/002234337100800201

Gao, X., & Zheng, Y. (2020). 'Heavy mountains' for Chinese humanities and social science academics in the quest for world-class universities. *Compare: A Journal of Comparative and International Education, 50*, 554–572. https://doi.org/10.1080/03057925.2018.1538770

Garrett, P. B., & Baquedano-López, P. (2002). Language socialization: Reproduction and continuity, transformation and change. *Annual Review of Anthropology, 31*, 339–361. https://doi.org/10.1146/annurev.anthro.31.040402.085352

Giroux, H. (2002). Neoliberalism, corporate culture, and the promise of higher education: The university as a democratic public sphere. *Harvard Educational Review, 72*, 425–464. https://doi.org/10.17763/haer.72.4.0515nr62324n71p1

Giroux, H. A. (2003). Selling out higher education. *Policy Futures in Education, 1*, 179–200. https://doi.org/10.2304/pfie.2003.1.1.6

Gosden, H. (1996). Verbal reports of Japanese novices' research writing practices in English. *Journal of Second Language Writing, 5*, 109–128. https://doi.org/10.1016/s1060-3743(96)90021-1

Gosden, H. (2003). 'Why not give us the full story?': Functions of referees' comments in peer reviews of scientific research papers. *Journal of English for Academic Purposes, 2*, 87–101. https://doi.org/10.1016/s1475-1585(02)00037-1

Hanauer, D. I., & Englander, K. (2013). *Scientific writing in a second language*. Parlor Press.

Harris, S. (2005). Rethinking academic identities in neo-liberal times. *Teaching in Higher Education, 10*, 421–433. https://doi.org/10.1080/13562510500238986

Harvey, D. (2005). *A brief history of neoliberalism*. Oxford University Press.

Harwood, N., & Hadley, G. (2004). Demystifying institutional practices: Critical pragmatism and the teaching of academic writing. *English for Specific Purposes, 23*, 355–377. https://doi.org/10.1016/s0889-4906(03)00058-9

Hasrati, M. (2013). Material and credentialing incentives as symbolic violence: Local engagement and global participation through joint publication. *Journal of Business and Technical Communication, 27*, 154–179. https://doi.org/10.1177/1050651912468886

Huang, J. C. (2010). Publishing and learning writing for publication in English: Perspectives of NNES PhD students in science. *Journal of English for Academic Purposes, 9*, 33–44. https://doi.org/10.1016/j.jeap.2009.10.001

Hyland, K. (2009). English for professional academic purposes: Writing for scholarly publication. In D. Belcher (Ed.), *English for Specific Purposes in theory and practice* (pp. 83–105). University of Michigan Press.

Hyland, K., & Hamp-Lyons, L. (2002). EAP: Issues and directions. *Journal of English for Academic Purposes, 1*, 1–12. https://doi.org/10.1016/s1475-1585(02)00002-4

Ivanič, R. (1998). *Writing and identity: The discoursal construction of identity in academic writing*. John Benjamins.

Ivanič, R. (2004). Discourses of writing and learning to write. *Language and Education, 18*, 220–245. https://doi.org/10.1080/09500780408666877

Johns, A. M. (1997). *Text, role and context: Developing academic literacies*. Cambridge University Press.

Kachru, B. B. (1986). *The alchemy of English: The spread, functions, and models of non-native Englishes*. Pergamon.

Kozulin, A. (1986). The concept of activity in Soviet psychology: Vygotsky, his disciples and critics. *American Psychologist, 41*, 264–274. https://doi.org/10.1037/0003-066x.41.3.264

Kubota, R. (2003). Striving for original voice in publication?: A critical reflection. In C. P. Casanave & S. Vandrick (Eds.), *Writing for scholarly publication: Behind the scenes in language education* (pp. 73–83). Lawrence Erlbaum.

Kuutti, K. (1996). Activity theory as a potential framework for human-computer interaction research. In B. A. Nardi (Ed.), *Context and consciousness: Activity theory and human-computer interaction* (pp. 17–44). MIT Press.

Lave, J., & Wenger, E. (1991). *Situated Learning: Legitimate peripheral participation*. Cambridge University Press.

Lee, S., & Roth, W.-M. (2003). Becoming and belonging: Learning qualitative research through legitimate peripheral participation. *Forum: Qualitative Social Research, 4*, Art. 35. http://nbn-resolving.de/urn:nbn:de:0114-fqs0302355

Lee, H., & Lee, K. (2013). Publish (in international indexed journals) or perish: Neoliberal ideology in a Korean university. *Language Policy, 12*, 215–230. https://doi.org/10.1007/s10993-012-9267-2

Lei, J., & Hu, G. (2015). Apprenticeship in scholarly publishing: A student perspective on doctoral supervisors' roles. *Publications, 3*, 27–42. https://doi.org/10.3390/publications3010027

Leont'ev, A. N. (1978/2009). *Activity, consciousness, and personality*. Marxists Internet Archive (Sourced from the edition published in 1978 by Prentice-Hall).

Leont'ev, A. N. (1981). The problem of activity in psychology. In J. V. Wertsch (Ed.), *The concept of activity in Soviet psychology* (pp. 37–71). Sharpe.

Li, Y. (2005). Multidimensional enculturation: The case of an EFL Chinese doctoral student. *Journal of Asian Pacific Communication, 15*, 153–170. https://doi.org/10.1075/japc.15.1.10li

Li, Y. (2006a). A doctoral student of physics writing for publication: A sociopolitically-oriented case study. *English for Specific Purposes, 25*, 456–478. https://doi.org/10.1016/j.esp.2005.12.002

Li, Y. (2006b). Negotiating knowledge contribution to multiple discourse communities: A doctoral student of computer science writing for publication. *Journal of Second Language Writing, 15*, 159–178. https://doi.org/10.1016/j.jslw.2006.07.001

Li, Y. (2007). Apprentice scholarly writing in a community of practice: An intraview of an NNES graduate student writing a research article. *TESOL Quarterly, 41*, 55–79. https://doi.org/10.1002/j.1545-7249.2007.tb00040.x

Li, Y. (2016). "Publish SCI papers or no degree": Practices of Chinese doctoral supervisors in response to the publication pressure on science students. *Asia Pacific Journal of Education, 36*, 545–558. https://doi.org/10.1080/02188791.2015.1005050

Li, Y., & Flowerdew, J. (2009). International engagement versus local commitment: Hong Kong academics in the humanities and social sciences writing for publication. *Journal of English for Academic Purposes, 8*, 279–293. https://doi.org/10.1016/j.jeap.2009.05.002

References

Li, Y., & Yang, R. (2018). Chinese business schools pursuing growth through international publishing: Evidence from institutional genres. In M. Curry & T. Lillis (Eds.), *Global academic publishing: Policies, perspectives, and pedagogies* (pp. 50–69). Multilingual Matters.

Lillis, T., & Curry, M. J. (2010). *Academic writing in a global context: The politics and practices of publishing in English*. Routledge.

Lillis, T. (2012). Economies of signs in writing for academic publication: The case of English medium 'national' journals. *Journal of Advanced Composition, 32*, 695–722.

Lillis, T., & Curry, M. J. (2006a). Professional academic writing by multilingual scholars: Interactions with literacy brokers in the production of English-medium texts. *Written Communication, 23*, 3–35. https://doi.org/10.1177/0741088305283754

Lillis, T., & Curry, M. J. (2006b). Reframing notions of competence in scholarly writing: From individual to networked activity. *Revista Canaria De Estudios Ingleses, 53*, 63–78.

Lillis, T. M., & Scott, M. (2007). Defining academic literacies research: Issues of epistemology, ideology and strategy. *Journal of Applied Linguistics, 4*, 5–32.

Liu, J. (2004). Co-constructing academic discourse from the periphery: Chinese applied linguistists' centripetal participation in scholarly publication. *Asian Journal of English Language Teaching, 14*, 1–22.

Lynch, K. (2015). Control by numbers: New managerialism and ranking in higher education. *Critical Studies in Education, 56*, 190–207. https://doi.org/10.1080/17508487.2014.949811

McKinley, J. (2015). Critical argument and writer Identity: Social constructivism as a theoretical framework for EFL academic writing. *Critical Inquiry in Language Studies, 12*, 184–207. https://doi.org/10.1080/15427587.2015.1060558

Morita, N., & Kobayashi, M. (2008). Academic discourse socialization in a second language. In P. A. Duff & N. H. Hornberger (Eds.), *Encyclopedia of language and education* (2nd ed., pp. 243–255). Springer.

Mu, C. (2020). *Understanding Chinese multilingual scholars' experiences of writing and publishing in English: A social-cognitive perspective*. Palgrave Macmillan.

Mu, C., & Zhang, L. J. (2018). Understanding Chinese multilingual scholars' experiences of publishing research in English. *Journal of Scholarly Publishing, 49*, 397–418. https://doi.org/10.3138/jsp.49.4.02

Myers, G. (1985). The social construction of two biologists' proposals. *Written Communication, 2*, 219–245. https://doi.org/10.1177/0741088385002003001

O'Regan, J. P., & Gray, J. (2018). The bureaucratic distortion of academic work: A transdisciplinary analysis of the UK Research Excellence Framework in the age of neoliberalism. *Language and Intercultural Communication, 18*, 533–548. https://doi.org/10.1080/14708477.2018.1501847

Olssen, M., & Peters, M. A. (2005). Neoliberalism, higher education and the knowledge economy: From the free market to knowledge capitalism. *Journal of Education Policy, 20*, 313–345. https://doi.org/10.1080/02680930500108718

Paltridge, B. (2004). Academic writing. *Language Teaching, 37*, 87–105. https://doi.org/10.1017/S0261444804002216

Prior, P. (1998). *Writing/Disciplinarity: A sociohistoric account of literate activity in the academy*. Lawrence Erlbaum.

Prior, P. (2003, March). *Are communities of practice really an alternative to discourse communities?* American Association of Applied Linguistics, Arlinton, VA.

Prior, P., & Bilbro, R. (2012). Academic enculturation: Developing literate practices and disciplinary identities. In M. Castelló & C. Donahue (Eds.), *University writing: Selves and texts in academic societies*. Emerald.

Rogoff, B. (1995). Observing sociocultural activity on three planes: Participatory appropriation, guided participation, and apprenticeship. In J. V. Wertsch, P. del Rio, & A. Alvarez (Eds.), *Sociocultural studies of mind* (pp. 139–164). Cambridge University Press.

Roth, W.-M. (2007). Heeding the unit of analysis. *Mind, Culture, and Activity, 14*, 143–149. https://doi.org/10.1080/10749030701316227

Roth, W.-M., & Lee, Y.-J. (2007). "Vygotsky's neglected legacy": Cultural-historical activity theory. *Review of Educational Research, 77*, 186–232. https://doi.org/10.3102/0034654306298273

Russell, D. R., & Yañez, A. (2003). "Big picture people rarely become historians": Genre systems and the contradictions of general education. In C. Bazerman & D. R. Russell (Eds.), *Writing selves/Writing societies: Research from activity perspectives* (pp. 331–362). The WAC Clearinghouse.

Salager-Meyer, F. (2008). Scientific publishing in developing countries: Challenges for the future. *Journal of English for Academic Purposes, 7*, 121–132. https://doi.org/10.1016/j.jeap.2008.03.009

Sandy, W., & Shen, H. (2019). Publish to earn incentives: How do Indonesian professors respond to the new policy?. *Higher Education, 77*, 247–263. https://doi.org/10.1007/s10734-018-0271-0

Schmeichel, M., Sharma, A., & Pittard, E. (2017). Contours of neoliberalism in US empirical educational research. *Curriculum Inquiry, 47*, 195–216. https://doi.org/10.1080/03626784.2017.1283592

Shi, L. (2003). Writing in two cultures: Chinese professors return from the west. *Canadian Modern Language Review, 59*, 369–391. https://doi.org/10.3138/cmlr.59.3.369

Smyth, J. (2017). *The toxic university: Zombie leadership, academic rock stars and neoliberal ideology*. Palgrave.

Starfield, S. (2007). New directions in student academic writing. In J. Cummins & C. Davison (Eds.), *International handbook of English language teaching* (pp. 875–890). Springer.

Storberg-Walker, J. (2008). Wenger's communities of practice revisited: A (failed?) exercise in applied communities of practice theory-building research. *Advances in Developing Human Resources, 10*, 555–577. https://doi.org/10.1177/1523422308319541

Suspitsyna, T. (2010). Accountability in American education as a rhetoric and a technology of governmentality. *Journal of Education Policy, 25*, 567–586. https://doi.org/10.1080/02680930903548411

Swales, J. (1990). *Genre analysis: English in academic and research settings*. Cambridge University Press.

Swales, J. (2004). *Research genres: Explorations and applications*. Oxford University Press.

Tang, R. (2012). The issues and challenges facing academic writers from ESL/EFL contexts: An overview. In R. Tang (Ed.), *Academic writing in a second or foreign language: Issues and challenges facing ESL/EFL academic writers in higher education contexts* (pp. 1–18). Continuum.

Tardy, C. M. (2006). Researching first and second language genre learning: A comparative review and a look ahead. *Journal of Second Language Writing, 15*, 79–101. https://doi.org/10.1016/j.jslw.2006.04.003

Tuomi-Gröhn, T., & Engeström, Y. (2007). Conceptualizing transfer: From standard notions to developmental perspectives. In T. Tuomi-Gröhn & Y. Engeström (Eds.), *Between school and work: New perspectives on transfer and boundary crossing* (pp. 19–38). Emerald.

Tuomi-Gröhn, T., Engeström, Y., & Young, M. (2007). From transfer to boundary-crossing between school and work as a tool for developing vocational education: An introduction. In T. Tuomi-Gröhn & Y. Engeström (Eds.), *Between school and work: New perspectives on transfer and boundary crossing* (pp. 1–15). Emerald.

Uzuner, S. (2008). Multilingual scholars' participation in core/global academic communities: A literature review. *Journal of English for Academic Purposes, 7*, 250–263. https://doi.org/10.1016/j.jeap.2008.10.007

Vygotsky, L. S. (1978). *Mind in society: The development of higher psychological processes*. Harvard University Press.

Vygotsky, L. S. (1981). The instrumental method in psychology. In J. V. Wertsch (Ed.), *The concept of activity in Soviet psychology* (pp. 134–143). Sharpe.

Wallerstein, I. M. (1991). *Geopolitics and geoculture: Essays on the changing world-system*. Cambridge University Press.

References

Watson, M. (Ed.). (2012). *Publication practices and multilingual professionals in US universities: Towards critical perspectives on administration and pedagogy.* The WAC Clearinghouse.

Wenger, E. (1998). *Communities of practice: Learning, meaning, and identity.* Cambridge University Press.

Witte, S. P., & Haas, C. (2005). Research in activity: An analysis of speed bumps as mediational means. *Written Communication, 22,* 127–165. https://doi.org/10.1177/0741088305274781

Woodward-Kron, R. (2004). 'Discourse communities' and 'writing apprenticeship': An investigation of these concepts in undergraduate education students' writing. *Journal of English for Academic Purposes, 3,* 139–161. https://doi.org/10.1016/j.jeap.2003.09.001

Chapter 3
Doctoral Publication Policies: Neoliberal Ideologies and Stakeholder Perspectives

As outlined in the previous two chapters, the aim of this book is to explore policies, practices, and identities pertaining to doctoral publication, and connections between them. This chapter examines institutional policies on doctoral publication and supervisor and doctoral student perspectives on those policies. By analysing the focal university's requirements and rewards schemes for doctoral publication, it reveals that the institutional policies subscribe to neoliberal ideologies, endorse market rationalities, and privilege managerial over professional values and practices. It also delves into supervisor and student perspectives on the institutional requirements and rewards schemes for doctoral publication, showing that the supervisor and doctoral students prioritise internal motivations over external material and symbolic rewards for publishing. These analyses elucidate (mis)alignments between institutional policies and stakeholder perspectives on doctoral publication. This chapter concludes with a critique of the (mis)alignments between institutional policies and stakeholder perspectives, and a discussion of the potential impacts of the institutional policies on doctoral students' publishing practices and evolving identities.

3.1 Institutional Policies on Doctoral Publication

In analysing the institutional documents on doctoral education and publication, a tension was identified between the managerial rationalities and practices espoused in the institutional policies on doctoral education and publication, and the professional beliefs and values undergirding the purported institutional objectives of doctoral education and publication.

The University Regulations for Doctoral Education spelt out expectations for doctoral degree recipients in the Programme Objectives section.[1] The stated objectives sought to graduate doctoral students with an array of qualities, including

> Have a broad and in-depth knowledge of the discipline under study and a good grasp of related disciplines; have the abilities to conduct academic research independently, teach at higher educational institutions, and serve as principal investigators for large-scale scientific research and technological development projects or for projects that explore and seek solutions to our country's economic and social problems; make a novel contribution to science or technology.

These objectives centre on two widely-recognised goals of doctoral education—the production of knowledge and the reproduction of knowledge producers (see, e.g., Aitchison et al., 2012; Boud & Lee, 2009; Delamont et al., 2000; Parry, 2007). As Kamler (2008) has observed, the production of new knowledge and the reproduction of knowledge contributors are "crucial outcome[s] of doctoral education" (292) because they encapsulate professional beliefs and values about doctoral education and constitute the cornerstone of doctoral education.

Despite these envisioned professional beliefs and values, what really undergirded the institutional policies on doctoral education and publication was managerial rationality that encouraged the use of measurable publication outputs to manage, regulate, and control doctoral students' learning and publishing practices. The University Regulations for Doctoral Education, for example, stipulated that

> To ensure the quality of the doctoral degree and step up the requirements for the award of the doctoral degree, schools and departments should gradually adopt the policy of awarding the graduation certificate and the doctoral degree separately. The publication requirements for doctoral students should comply with the University Regulations for the Award of Degrees.[2]

These university-wide regulations aside, each school and department had their own publishing requirements. For example, in addition to the general guideline about publishing at least one SCI journal article noted above, the School of Medicine had an in-house document that laid out the publishing requirements for its doctoral students:

> The graduation certificate and the doctoral degree are awarded separately. To be awarded the doctoral degree, candidates must meet the following requirements:
>
> 1. Ph.D. students must publish at least one first-author article in an SCI journal (if the supervisor is the first author and the student is the second author, they must publish at least two articles in SCI journals);
>
> ...
>
> 2. An article published in a journal with an impact factor higher than 5.0 can be counted towards the fulfillment of the publication requirements for two doctoral students (both

---

[1] The document quoted here comprises nine sections, including Programme Objectives, Programme of Study and Individual Study Plans, Mode of Study, Length of Study, Areas of Research, Required Coursework, Course Examinations, Thesis Proposal Defence, and Research and Thesis.

[2] Universities in Chinese mainland award both a graduation certificate and a degree to students in degree programmes who meet all of the university's graduation requirements. The requirements for obtaining the degree are usually higher than those for attaining the graduation certificate. For example, students who have flunked a certain number of courses or failed to meet the university's publication requirements can get only the graduation certificates but not the degrees.

3.1 Institutional Policies on Doctoral Publication

students are co-first authors). An article published in a journal with an impact factor higher than 7.0 can be counted towards the fulfillment of the publication requirements for three doctoral students (all the three students are co-first authors). An article published in *Nature* or *Science* can be counted towards the fulfillment of the publication requirements for ten doctoral students. All the candidates who apply for the award of the doctoral degree based on the same publication must have made substantive contributions to the research reported in the publication….;

3. All the above publications must list the university as the first affiliation.

….

("Requirements for Thesis Research and Scholarly Publishing Concerning the Application for the Doctoral Degree")

These requirements clearly demonstrate managerial accountability designed to quantify, manage, and audit doctoral students' publication outputs. In the name of quality assurance, the institutional publication requirements linked the award of doctoral degrees directly to publication outputs. To that end, a performance target (i.e., one first-authored SCI paper) was established and measures were accordingly developed to audit doctoral students' performances and hold them accountable for their performances. These regulations are obviously characteristic of a managerial accountability regime (Connell, 2013; Olssen & Peters, 2005; Suspitsyna, 2010). In addition, by specifying performance targets in terms of numbers of publications and impact factors of journals, the regulations sought to improve productivity through target setting, performance evaluating, and results auditing. These productivity-enhancing practices epitomise managerial accountability (Mahony & Weiner, 2017; Ranson, 2003).

Moreover, the regulations commodified doctoral students' publications by assigning differential 'exchange value' to articles published in journals with different impact factors and ignoring research articles published in non-indexed journals (Curry & Lillis, 2018; Englander & Uzuner-Smith, 2013; Holborow, 2015). Finally, the regulations prioritised measurable outputs over knowledge production practices and scholarly publishing experiences. For instance, while encouraging doctoral students to collaborate with supervisors and fellow students, the regulations provided no guidelines for doing that. It is thus evident that these regulations were primarily driven by managerial rationality instead of professional rationality (Connell, 2013; Olssen & Peters, 2005; Suspitsyna, 2010).

The market-driven managerial rationality was also evident in the institutional rewards systems for doctoral publication. First and foremost, the School of Medicine instituted the SCI Publication Foundation in the early 2000s that incentivized researchers to publish in SCI journals through monetary rewards. The amount of money awarded for each SCI paper depended on the impact factor of the journal in which the paper was published, ranging from 10,000 RMB (US$1612) for an abstract appearing in an SCI journal with an impact factor lower than 1 to 160,000 RMB (US$25,793) for a full-length empirical article or a review article in an SCI journal with an impact factor higher than 10 ("Regulations on the Management of the SCI Publication Foundation"). The foundation rewarded the staff and students with research grants that were supposed to be used for research purposes only, such as paying for research personnel or purchasing experimental materials and equipment. Additionally, supervisors could also use the foundation grant to pay their doctoral students a monthly allowance of no more than 800 RMB (US$129) for their assistance with research or teaching.

In addition to the SCI Publication Foundation, as Professor Liu pointed out, the university had also put various other rewards schemes in place to specifically incentivise students to publish in international journals, including the award of conference funding, the eligibility for the National Scholarships for Graduate Students (a prestigious annual award of 30,000RMB [US$4835] for each winner), places on honour lists, outstanding research awards, converting from master's to doctoral candidature, and eligibility to apply for the baccalaureate-Ph.D. programme.[3] Professor Liu went on to reveal that a candidate's research output as measured by the number and impact factors of her or his SCI publications often constituted "the main determining factor" in selecting recipients for those rewards. She further noted that schools and departments also had their own incentive schemes to encourage students to publish in international journals. The School of Medicine, for example, had launched a prestigious annual Best New Researchers award to commend doctoral students who did outstanding research. The award rewarded ten doctoral students and their supervisors with 10,000 RMB (US$1612) each per annum.

Moreover, the School of Medicine had a performance-based scholarships system as well,[4] which drew on several sources of funding, including tuition fees waivers from the university, national student aid from the Ministry of Education, and research and teaching assistantships from the university, hospital, and supervisor. The scholarships were divided into four classes, namely, first-class, second-class, and third-class scholarships, and student aid and assistantship only. While all full-time doctoral students were eligible for the first three classes of scholarships, part-time students could receive only the student aid and assistantship. The four classes of scholarships provided an annual stipend of around 58,000 RMB (US$9347), 49,000 RMB (US$7897), 42,000 RMB (US$6769), and 24,000 RMB (US$3868), respectively. About 15%, 70%, 10%, and 5% of each cohort received the first-class, second-class, and third-class scholarships, and the student aid and assistantship only, respectively, at the time of admission based on their performances in the entrance examinations and interviews. Further, at the end of their second year, their scholarships were to be renewed based on their performances during their first one and a half years into the programme. The assessment of their performances consisted of their supervisors' appraisal of their progress in research and coursework.

It is thus clear that these rewards schemes entail various neoliberal ideologies and subordinate professional logics and values to market logics and values. First, the

---

[3] The baccalaureate-Ph.D. programme refers to direct doctoral programme admission, i.e., students entering the doctoral programme directly from baccalaureate studies rather than from master's studies.

[4] This scholarships scheme followed the university's scholarships scheme, though it was slightly more generous than that of the university.

university and the school instituted the rewards schemes to increase doctoral students' publication outputs, reflecting a market-driven logic that competition improves productivity (Ball, 2003; Mahony & Weiner, 2017). Second, the awards as well as the performance-based scholarships involved regular checking, monitoring, and auditing of doctoral students' publication outputs (Gao & Zheng, 2020; Olssen & Peters, 2005; Suspitsyna, 2010), which are typical of a market-driven auditing culture. Third, publication outputs were regarded as commodities with material and symbolic values (Curry & Lillis, 2018; Englander & Uzuner-Smith, 2013; Holborow, 2015). Fourth, and relatedly, the rewards schemes prioritised the exchange value over the use value of doctoral publications as they placed higher value on SCI publications and ascribed lower value or even no value to non-SCI publications (Curry & Lillis, 2018; Feng et al., 2013; Lee & Lee, 2013; Lillis, 2012).

3.2 Supervisor and Student Perspectives

The quality assurance rationality and the market-driven logic found in the university's policy documents were also manifested in supervisor and student perspectives on scholarly publishing during doctoral study. First, the participants appeared to endorse the university's publication requirements, holding that they were meant to maintain the quality of the doctoral programme and degree. Professor Liu, for example, pointed out that "although there are a lot of controversies over the policy of 'publish or no degree', I think the current policy is necessary if we are to facilitate students' scholarly publishing efforts and enhance the quality of the doctoral programme" (Interview). Similarly, Xiao noted that "I think the requirement is feasible and reasonable for doctoral students" (interview via QQ). However, given the high stakes of graduation, the supervisor's and the doctoral students' most immediate and urgent motive for publishing was, not surprisingly, to meet the university's publication requirements for graduation. As Professor Liu observed, "of course, students are concerned most about graduation [meeting the university's publication requirements for graduation]" (Interview). Likewise, Cui and Dong characterised the goal of on-time graduation with the degree as "the greater good" (*zongti dade liyi*, literally the overall greater interest/good) and 'the primary target' (*yiji mubiao*, literally the first-order objectives), respectively (Interview). As will be illustrated in Chap. 4, this overriding emphasis on the product and outcome of scholarly publishing and doctoral education had a great bearing on the doctoral students' scholarly publishing practices.

In contrast to their embracing of the institutional publication requirements and neoliberal ideologies underlying them, the supervisor and the students held only a tepid attitude towards the institutional rewards schemes. Professor Liu, for example, observed that "external incentives are not the most important and what's the most important is students' inner drives" (Interview). She went on to explain that

> The university's rewards schemes can provide students with some incentives to publish in international journals. But what's more important for them is they can develop their abilities

through that. Any external material rewards pale in comparison to their acquired abilities, which cannot be taken away. (Interview)

The students largely shared Professor Liu's view on the rewards scheme. They saw the material and symbolic rewards primarily as by-products of fulfilling the publication requirements and attached greater importance to such internal rewards as learning and career development. When queried about her views on the university's publication requirements, Wei expressed unreserved approval, noting that "publishing more English journal articles can help us improve our English and benefit our future careers in various ways" (Interview). Similarly, Fang observed that "my experience publishing English journal articles is very important to me because I learned from it about how to publish in English journals" (Interview). Likewise, Xiao viewed publishing English journal articles as "an exercise and a way to improve [herself]" (Interview). Further, while appreciating the external incentives, the participants in this study seemed to privilege the internal incentives of learning scholarly publishing and becoming members of the academic community. These views echo those of the professors at a Korean university in Lee and Lee's (2013) study, and prioritise "the internal goods of motivation to improve" over the external goods of material and symbolic rewards in realising and fostering achievement (Ranson, 2003, p. 473).

Furthermore, the university's publication requirements faced even clear resistance because they valued international publications over local publications. As Liang pointed out, although she would like to write and publish more in Chinese because of her desire to help practitioners and patients, the university's publication requirements discouraged her from doing that. In her own words,

I want to share my research with people who are really concerned about it. My research investigates the life rebuilding of disaster survivors, so I would like to make the results available to my colleagues who are doing similar research or who are involved in the rebuilding work. So if I publish my research in English, perhaps only the international readership that has access to it would pay attention to it. By contrast, those in our society who we need to call on to take actions may not have access to it. I think that's a pity. (Liang, Interview)

Liang's quandary on whether to publish her research in English or in Chinese exemplified the tension between the doctoral students' aspirations to contribute knowledge to the local community and the university's demands on publishing in SCI (international) journals. This conundrum has been extensively discussed in the literature (see, e.g., Curry & Lillis, 2013; Duszak & Lewkowicz, 2008; Flowerdew & Li, 2009a; Lillis & Curry, 2010), raising questions about the hegemonic role of English as an academic lingua franca and its pernicious influences on local languages, scholarship, and research cultures. Liang's account also demonstrated "the tensions between the logic of managerial control and the conventions of professional autonomy" (Deem, 1998, p. 52). Specifically, her professional autonomy in deciding where to publish her research was at odds with the university's managerial control over where doctoral students should publish their research. It would not be unreasonable to anticipate that the university's managerial control would probably prevail over her professional autonomy because the former would determine if and when she could graduate. As a result, as Chaps. 4 and 5 will show, the university's publication requirements managed, regulated, and reshaped doctoral students' publishing practices and evolving identities (Ball, 2003; Deem, 1998, 2004; Lynch, 2015).

3.3 (Dis)connections Between Institutional Policies and Stakeholder Perspectives

The above analyses showed both connections and disconnections between institutional policies and stakeholder perspectives on doctoral publication. The university and the major stakeholders appeared to hold multiple and heterogeneous motives for scholarly publishing during doctoral candidature, including ensuring the quality of the doctoral programme and degree, meeting the university's publication requirements, fostering the doctoral students' scholarly abilities, preparing them for their future careers, and contributing to knowledge. These motives revolve around the dual goals of doctoral education, namely, the production of knowledge and the reproduction of researchers (Aitchison et al., 2012; Boud & Lee, 2009; Delamont et al., 2000; Kamler, 2008; Kandiko & Kinchin, 2012; McGrail et al., 2006; Parry, 2007). Kandiko and Kinchin (2012), for example, view doctoral education as "both a process of learning (for the student and the supervisor) and a product of a research project" (p. 3).

However, although the university and the stakeholders shared the long-term collective goals for scholarly publishing, they placed differing values on the product-related and the process-related motives. Specifically, while the university appeared to put an overriding emphasis on the product and outcome of scholarly publishing—prompt publications and timely graduation of doctoral students, the supervisor and doctoral students tended to prioritise the process and experience of scholarly publishing—learning, career preparation, and knowledge contribution. The prevalent emphasis on the product and outcome was most pronounced in the university's publication requirements and rewards schemes. The university's publication requirements, for example, were framed by the university as a mechanism to ensure the quality of the doctoral programme and degree (see Lee & Kamler, 2008). In this sense, the university seemed to use the publication requirements as "a stick" to push the doctoral students to meet the desired quality of its doctoral education and, consequently and concomitantly, boost its research profile. Because of the publication requirements, the doctoral students had to publish during their candidature in order to graduate with the degree. In so doing, they assumed the roles of both student researchers and expert researchers.

As will be explicated in detail in Chap. 5, this duality of the doctoral students' roles constituted a primary contradiction in their scholarly publishing activity systems and posed great challenges for them in their scholarly publishing activities. This "stick" approach may have to do with the intensifying institutionalisation of scholarly publishing as a graduation requirement for doctoral students in many countries (Casanave, 2010; Li, 2016) and the increasingly common quality assessment and assurance exercises imposed on universities by governments (Aitchison et al., 2012; Boud & Lee, 2009; Lee & Lee, 2013; Sinclair et al., 2014). As Raddon (2011) points out, "the value of research and writing has shifted from a knowledge-generating activity to one of impact and, indeed, of surveillance within the research community" (p. 40).

If the publication requirements functioned as "a stick" to push the doctoral students to publish, the rewards schemes instituted by the university served as "a carrot" to pull them to be productive. While previous research has documented rewards schemes for university faculty members (Braine, 2005; Duszak & Lewkowicz, 2008; Flowerdew & Li, 2009a; Huang, 2010, 2011, 2014; Lee & Lee, 2013; Li, 2006a; Li & Flowerdew, 2009; Lillis & Curry, 2010), relatively little has been reported about rewards aimed at encouraging doctoral students to publish. As pointed out earlier, the university had introduced various rewards schemes to encourage its doctoral students to publish and most of them were related to monetary rewards. Similar to those reported in previous research involving faculty members, these schemes reflect a performativity and audit culture characterised by an emphasis on performance and efficiency in the higher education sector. The premium placed on performance and efficiency may be attributed to the ever-accelerating globalisation and marketisation of the higher education sector over the past few decades (Aitchison et al., 2010; Lee & Lee, 2013; Sinclair et al., 2014; Starfield, 2004).

As a result of this overriding emphasis on performance and efficiency, research products and outcomes are increasingly taking precedence over research processes and experiences (McCormack, 2004; Paré, 2010; Raddon, 2011). Raddon (2011), for example, observes that "the value of research is located in performance, outcome and output rather than through research-as-process and knowledge-building" (p. 42). In such a research culture, "[research students] are expected to proceed steadily along their chosen path with their focus on the product rather than the process" (McCormack, 2004, p. 320). As will be illustrated in Chap. 4, the practices of the university and supervisors emphasised even more overwhelmingly the deliverables of scholarly publishing. Such policies and practices prioritised the product and outcome of scholarly publishing and tended to undermine doctoral students' learning experiences and knowledge contributions. Specifically, as will be discussed in Chap. 4, the prevailing product-oriented approach to scholarly publishing led the doctoral students to adopt the strategies of "starting early" and "orchestrating one's own research and publications with those of others." While effective in securing the product, these strategies constrained the doctoral students' opportunities to learn scholarly publishing.

Further, the above analyses revealed two primary contradictions in the doctoral students' scholarly publishing activity system within the doctoral study activity system: the duality of the object of developing the doctoral students into autonomous researchers while timely graduating them and having their knowledge contributions published (Tension A1 in Fig. 3.1); and the duality of the doctoral students' roles as student and expert researchers (Tension A2 in Fig. 3.1, see Table 3.1 for a summary

3.3 (Dis)connections Between Institutional Policies and Stakeholder …

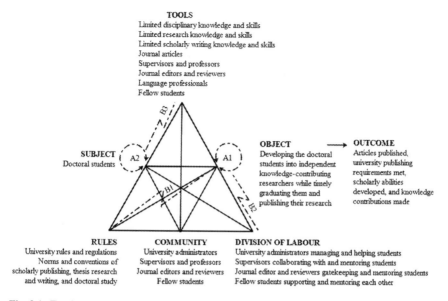

Fig. 3.1 Tensions concerning scholarly publishing within the doctoral study activity system

of these and other contradictions).[5] While the primary contradiction within the object component (A1) gave rise to and was manifested in the object-rules-related (B1) and object-roles-related (B2) secondary contradictions, the primary contradiction (A2) within the subject component led to and was reflected in the subject-tools-related secondary contradiction (B3).

As will be explicated in Chap. 4, the object-rules-related contradiction was concerned with the tension between attaining the object of the scholarly publishing activity system and meeting the competing demands emanating from the doctoral study activity system in a tight timeframe (Tension B1 in Fig. 3.1). It was most saliently reflected in the time pressure that all of the student participants reported facing in meeting the institutional publication requirements within their stringent doctoral candidature. To overcome this contradiction, the doctoral students resorted to "starting early" and/or "orchestrating one's own research and publishing activities with those of others", which, though capable of ameliorating the tension, tended to lead to new contradictions (see Chap. 4 for details). The object-roles-related contradiction had to do with the tension between the object of the scholarly publishing activity system and the roles (or division of labour) of the university and supervisor as managers of the product/outcome of the doctoral students' scholarly publishing activity rather than as mentors for (the process of) developing their scholarly abilities (Tension B2 in Fig. 3.1). This contradiction was most pronounced in the inadequate

---

[5] In this book, the letters of A, B, C, and D refer to primary, secondary, tertiary, and quaternary contradictions, respectively.

Table 3.1 A summary of the activity systems and thematic analyses of the doctoral students' challenges and contradictions in scholarly publishing

Contradictions (activity system analysis)		Challenges/difficulties (thematic analysis)
Arose from (primary contradictions)	Manifested in (secondary contradictions)	
Object-Object: The duality of the object of developing the doctoral students into autonomous researchers while timely graduating them and having their knowledge contributions published	**Object-Rules**: The tension between attaining the object of developing the doctoral students into autonomous researchers and the expectations of meeting the competing demands of doctoral study within a tight timeframe	Time pressure
	Object-Division of Labour: The tension between attaining the object of developing the doctoral students into autonomous researchers and the roles of the university and supervisor as managers of the outcome of the doctoral students' scholarly publishing activity rather than as mentors for (the process of) developing their scholarly abilities	Inadequate institutional and supervisory support (little ongoing scholarly writing support from both the university and the supervisor)
Subject-Subject: The duality of the doctoral students' roles as student and expert researchers	**Subject-Tools**: The tension in the doctoral students' developing but still limited grasp and use of various conceptual tools needed for successful scholarly publishing	Limited language skills Unfamiliarity with the rules of the scholarly publishing game • Difficulties in selecting appropriate journals • Difficulties in responding appropriately and effectively to journal editors and reviewers Inadequate knowledge and skills for conceptualising and designing research: • Difficulties in selecting publishable research topics • Difficulties in choosing appropriate research methodology

institutional and supervisory support reported by some doctoral students for their scholarly publishing activities.

Finally, as will be illustrated in Chap. 5, the subject-tools-related contradiction pertained to the tension in the doctoral students' developing but still limited grasp and use of various conceptual tools needed for successful scholarly publishing (Tension B3 in Fig. 3.1) and was manifested in the doctoral students' difficulties in using various conceptual tools (e.g., language, target journal selection, and knowledge and skills of negotiating with journal editors and reviewers, research topic selection) that were crucial for successful scholarly publishing. To tackle this contradiction, the doctoral students turned to an array of mediating resources, including both cultural artefacts and social others, which helped them not only mitigate those tensions but also move towards increasingly fuller participation in the scholarly publishing activity system.

3.4 Conclusion

This chapter has explored institutional policies on doctoral publication and supervisor and doctoral student perspectives on those policies. First, it has revealed neoliberal ideologies underlying the institutional requirements and rewards schemes for doctoral publication, including the commodification of doctoral publications, the managerial accountability, and the auditing culture. In particular, it has uncovered a tension between the purported institutional professional objectives of doctoral education and publication—production of knowledge and reproduction of knowledge producers—and the externally imposed objectives of institutional requirements and incentives for publication that are characterised by measuring, regulating, and controlling doctoral students' publication outputs. This finding indicates the privileging of the managerial accountability over the professional accountability in the institutional requirements for doctoral education and publication.

Second, it has also shown that the various institutional rewards schemes intended to induce doctoral students to publish during candidature tended to exacerbate the already prevailing market-driven neoliberal ideologies underlying the university's publication requirements and "distor[t] the space in which doctoral work is done and research careers are forged" (Aitchison et al., 2010, p. 2). Third, it has unveiled that while appreciating the institutional rewards schemes, the supervisor and doctoral students seemed to place a higher value on such internal rewards as learning, becoming members of the academic community, and contributing knowledge to the local community. This suggests that there are both connections and disconnections between the institutional policies on doctoral publication and the supervisor and student perspectives thereon. Finally, it has indicated that the misalignments between institutional policies and stakeholder perspectives on doctoral publication may impinge on both students' publishing practices and evolving identities, as will be discussed in detail in Chaps. 4 and 5, respectively.

References

Aitchison, C., Kamler, B., & Lee, A. (2010a). Introduction: Why publishing pedagogies? In C. Aitchison, B. Kamler, & A. Lee (Eds.), *Publishing pedagogies for the doctorate and beyond* (pp. 1–11). Routledge.

Aitchison, C., Catterall, J., Ross, P., & Burgin, S. (2012). 'Tough love and tears': Learning doctoral writing in the sciences. *Higher Education Research & Development, 31*, 435–447. https://doi.org/10.1080/07294360.2011.559195

Ball, S. J. (2003). The teacher's soul and the terrors of performativity. *Journal of Education Policy, 18*, 215–228. https://doi.org/10.1080/0268093022000043065

Boud, D., & Lee, A. (2009). Introduction. In D. Boud & A. Lee (Eds.), *Changing practices of doctoral education* (pp. 1–9). Routledge.

Braine, G. (2005). The challenge of academic publishing: A Hong Kong perspective. *TESOL Quarterly, 39*, 707–716. https://doi.org/10.2307/3588528

Casanave, C. P. (2010). Dovetailing under impossible circumstances. In C. Aitchison, B. Kamler, & A. Lee (Eds.), *Publishing pedagogies for the doctorate and beyond* (pp. 47–63). Routledge.

Connell, R. (2013). The neoliberal cascade and education: An essay on the market agenda and its consequences. *Critical Studies in Education, 54*(2), 99–112. https://doi.org/10.1080/17508487.2013.776990

Curry, M. J., & Lillis, T. (2013). Introduction to the thematic issue: Participating in academic publishing—consequences of linguistic policies and practices. *Language Policy, 12*, 209–213. https://doi.org/10.1007/s10993-013-9286-7

Curry, M. J., & Lillis, T. (2018). Problematising English as the privileged language of global academic publishing. In M. J. Curry & T. Lillis (Eds.), *Global academic publishing: Policies, perspectives, and pedagogies* (pp. 1–20). Multilingual Matters.

Deem, R. (1998). 'New managerialism' and higher education: The management of performances and cultures in universities in the United Kingdom. *International Studies in Sociology of Education, 8*, 47–70. https://doi.org/10.1080/0962021980020014

Deem, R. (2004). The knowledge worker, the manager-academic and the contemporary UK University: New and old forms of public management? *Financial Accountability & Management, 20*, 107–128. https://doi.org/10.1111/j.1468-0408.2004.00189.x

Delamont, S., Atkinson, P., & Parry, O. (2000). *The doctoral experience: Success and failure in graduate school*. Falmer Press.

Duszak, A., & Lewkowicz, J. (2008). Publishing academic texts in English: A Polish perspective. *Journal of English for Academic Purposes, 7*, 108–120. https://doi.org/10.1016/j.jeap.2008.03.001

Englander, K., & Uzuner-Smith, S. (2013). The role of policy in constructing the peripheral scientist in the era of globalization. *Language Policy, 12*, 231–250. https://doi.org/10.1007/s10993-012-9268-1

Feng, H., Beckett, G., & Huang, D. (2013). From 'import' to 'import—export' oriented internationalization: The impact of national policy on scholarly publication in China. *Language Policy, 12*, 251–272. https://doi.org/10.1007/s10993-013-9285-8

Flowerdew, J., & Li, Y. (2009). English or Chinese? The trade off between local and international publication among Chinese academics in the humanities and social sciences. *Journal of Second Language Writing, 18*, 1–16. https://doi.org/10.1016/j.jslw.2008.09.005

Gao, X., & Zheng, Y. (2020). 'Heavy mountains' for Chinese humanities and social science academics in the quest for world-class universities. *Compare: A Journal of Comparative and International Education, 50*, 554–572. https://doi.org/10.1080/03057925.2018.1538770

Huang, J. C. (2010). Publishing and learning writing for publication in English: Perspectives of NNES PhD students in science. *Journal of English for Academic Purposes, 9*, 33–44. https://doi.org/10.1016/j.jeap.2009.10.001

References

Huang, J. C. (2011). Attitudes of Taiwanese scholars toward English and Chinese as languages of publication. *Asia Pacific Journal of Education, 31*, 115–128. https://doi.org/10.1080/02188791.2011.566983

Huang, J. C. (2014). Learning to write for publication in English through genre-based pedagogy: A case in Taiwan. *System, 45*, 175–186. https://doi.org/10.1016/j.system.2014.05.010

Holborow, M. (2015). *Language and neoliberalism*. Routledge.

Kamler, B. (2008). Rethinking doctoral publication practices: Writing from and beyond the thesis. *Studies in Higher Education, 33*, 283–294. https://doi.org/10.1080/03075070802049236

Kandiko, C. B., & Kinchin, I. M. (2012). What is a doctorate? A concept-mapped analysis of process versus product in the supervision of lab-based PhDs. *Educational Research, 54*, 3–16. https://doi.org/10.1080/00131881.2012.658196

Lee, A., & Kamler, B. (2008). Bringing pedagogy to doctoral publishing. *Teaching in Higher Education, 13*, 511–523. https://doi.org/10.1080/13562510802334723

Lee, H., & Lee, K. (2013). Publish (in international indexed journals) or perish: Neoliberal ideology in a Korean university. *Language Policy, 12*, 215–230. https://doi.org/10.1007/s10993-012-9267-2

Li, Y. (2006). A doctoral student of physics writing for publication: A sociopolitically-oriented case study. *English for Specific Purposes, 25*, 456–478. https://doi.org/10.1016/j.esp.2005.12.002

Li, Y. (2016). "Publish SCI papers or no degree": Practices of Chinese doctoral supervisors in response to the publication pressure on science students. *Asia Pacific Journal of Education, 36*, 545–558. https://doi.org/10.1080/02188791.2015.1005050

Li, Y., & Flowerdew, J. (2009). International engagement versus local commitment: Hong Kong academics in the humanities and social sciences writing for publication. *Journal of English for Academic Purposes, 8*, 279–293. https://doi.org/10.1016/j.jeap.2009.05.002

Lillis, T. (2012). Economies of signs in writing for academic publication: The case of English medium "national" journals. *Journal of Advanced Composition, 32*, 695–722.

Lillis, T., & Curry, M. J. (2010). *Academic writing in a global context: The politics and practices of publishing in English*. Routledge.

Lynch, K. (2015). Control by numbers: New managerialism and ranking in higher education. *Critical Studies in Education, 56*, 190–207. https://doi.org/10.1080/17508487.2014.949811

Mahony, P., & Weiner, G. (2017). Neo-liberalism and the state of higher education in the UK. *Journal of Further and Higher Education*, 1–13. https://doi.org/10.1080/0309877x.2017.1378314

McCormack, C. (2004). Tensions between student and institutional conceptions of postgraduate research. *Studies in Higher Education, 29*, 319–334. https://doi.org/10.1080/0307507041000182600

McGrail, M. R., Rickard, C. M., & Jones, R. (2006). Publish or perish: A systematic review of interventions to increase academic publication rates. *Higher Education Research & Development, 25*, 19–35. https://doi.org/10.1080/07294360500453053

Olssen, M., & Peters, M. A. (2005). Neoliberalism, higher education and the knowledge economy: From the free market to knowledge capitalism. *Journal of Education Policy, 20*, 313–345. https://doi.org/10.1080/02680930500108718

Paré, A. (2010). Slow the presses: Concerns for premature publication. In C. Aitchison, B. Kamler, & A. Lee (Eds.), *Publishing pedagogies for the doctorate and beyond* (pp. 30–46). Routledge.

Parry, S. (2007). *Disciplines and doctorates: Higher education dynamics*. Springer.

Raddon, A. E. (2011). A changing environment: Narratives of learning about research. *International Journal for Researcher Development, 2*, 26–45. https://doi.org/10.1108/17597511111178005

Ranson, S. (2003). Public accountability in the age of neo-liberal governance. *Journal of Education Policy, 18*, 459–480. https://doi.org/10.1080/0268093032000124848

Sinclair, J., Barnacle, R., & Cuthbert, D. (2014). How the doctorate contributes to the formation of active researchers: What the research tells us. *Studies in Higher Education, 39*, 1972–1986. https://doi.org/10.1080/03075079.2013.806460

Starfield, S. (2004). 'Why does this feel empowering?': Thesis writing, concordancing, and the corporatizing university. In B. Norton & K. Toohey (Eds.), *Critical pedagogies and language learning* (pp. 138–157). Cambridge University Press.

Suspitsyna, T. (2010). Accountability in American education as a rhetoric and a technology of governmentality. *Journal of Education Policy, 25*, 567–586. https://doi.org/10.1080/02680930903548411

Chapter 4
Doctoral Publication Practices: Competing Demands and Coping Strategies

Chapter 3 has examined institutional policies and supervisor and student perspectives on doctoral publication, identified (mis)alignments between institutional policies and stakeholder perspectives, and divulged two primary contradictions inherent in the doctoral publication activity system. This chapter addresses the duality of the object—developing the doctoral students into autonomous researchers while timely graduating them and having their knowledge contributions published. It discusses the time pressure arising from the institutional publication requirements and explicates the two main strategies adopted by the students to cope with the time pressure. It then examines the managerial roles of the university and supervisor in the doctoral students' scholarly publishing activities. This chapter argues that the time pressure stemming from the institutional publication requirements tended to transform the doctoral students' scholarly publishing practices and truncate their experiences of scholarly publishing and learning.

4.1 Boundary Crossing Through Starting Early

The doctoral students in this study had to complete the required coursework, pass thesis proposal defence, publish an SCI journal article to meet the university's publication requirements, and write up and defend their thesis. The doctoral candidature at the university normally lasted three years, although candidates could apply for an extension of no more than three years. Given the relatively short candidature, not surprisingly, the university's publication requirements placed the doctoral students under tremendous time pressure. As Fang noted, "I feel our university has too stringent publication requirements. We are required to publish before we can graduate. I think that is too rigid (laughs). ... Time is too pressing!" (Interview). Liang concurred with Fang, noting that "if you consider the whole process of publishing an SCI article, it's really difficult to achieve that within the three-year candidature" (Interview).

In view of the time pressure, all of the participants placed a high value on the strategy of starting early in meeting the university's publication requirements. Fang admonished that on-time graduation with the degree hinged upon starting early: "If you want to graduate on time, you've got to start early" (Interview). Similarly, Cui pointed out that "you've got to start writing as soon as you have some data" (Interview). Professor Liu also exhorted that "they must start early if they want to graduate on time" (Interview). In response to such pressure, the doctoral students in this study started early either by working on the research data from their master's study (Xiao) or professional work (Fang), or by translating their course assignments into scholarly publications (Liang). From an activity theory perspective, the outcomes of the master's study, professional work, and coursework activity system served as tools for the scholarly publishing activity system (Casanave, 2010; Lundell & Beach, 2003; see also Barab et al., 2002; Hasu & Engeström, 2000; Miettinen, 2005).

Xiao wrote up an English manuscript during her master's study and the manuscript had gone through one round of review at the time of her enrolment in the Ph.D. programme. This head start placed her in an advantageous position because with that experience, she started to work on her second English manuscript based on some data provided by Professor Liu not long after her enrolment. Unlike Xiao, Fang followed one of her seniors' suggestions about starting early and took the strategy to the extreme by collecting data and finishing writing up two English manuscripts while she was working as a nurse at a hospital and before she was enrolled in the Ph.D. programme. Consequently, Xiao secured four SCI journal articles during her candidature, and according to Professor Liu and several of her fellow students, she graduated as the most successful doctoral student in the department. Similarly, Fang managed to publish one of her two manuscripts before the end of her candidature and the other one not long after her graduation. There is no doubt that Xiao's and Fang's early starts played an important role in their successful publication, though other factors, as will be elaborated below, might also have contributed to their successes.

Further, and more related to the doctoral study activity system, Professor Liu urged her doctoral students to start early by "integrating their scholarly publishing efforts with course assignments" (Interview). Specifically, she suggested that

> They should start writing while they are doing their coursework because they will be extremely busy once they begin their thesis research. They've got to make the most out of that period of time and integrate their scholarly writing with course assignments as some courses require written assignments. (Professor Liu, Interview)

Contrary to Professor Liu's perceived potential of translating course assignments into scholarly publications, the doctoral students expressed overall reservations about possible contributions of the coursework activity system to the scholarly publishing activity system. For one thing, as acknowledged by Professor Liu in the above excerpt, the coursework activity system and the thesis research activity system, particularly its subsidiary activity system of thesis proposal defence, tended to compete against the scholarly publishing activity system for the doctoral students' limited time. For another, the university's regulations and guidelines about coursework, especially the exam-oriented assessment methods, tended to curtail the students' opportunities

4.1 Boundary Crossing Through Starting Early

to translate course assignments into scholarly publications. Although some courses at the university required students to submit written assignments, those assignments were written in Chinese and did not contribute directly to the development of students' English scholarly publishing abilities or the fulfilment of the university's graduation requirements (see below Liang's case). For example, while one of the two specialisation courses taken by Dong asked students to write a literature review in Chinese, the other one required them to take a written examination. By contrast, Cui and Liang, who were in the joint-degrees programme, reported having done extensive written assignments and benefited greatly from them at the partner university. In contrasting the roles of written assignments and examinations in fostering students' writing abilities, Cui noted that

> Written assignments can better facilitate students' writing abilities than examinations. If we're required to sit in an examination, what we learn is 'dead' knowledge, which is of little value. So I think it's more valuable to write something, either full-length articles or sections of articles. (Interview via QQ)

As both Cui and Liang observed, most courses offered by the partner university required two written assignments. For example, the course on writing research articles asked students to write an introduction section and a methods section of a journal article. They both acknowledged that their experiences of writing course assignments at the partner university helped them improve their English scholarly writing abilities. However, despite the benefits of the course assignments at the partner university, neither of them was able to translate any of their assignments into publications.

Indeed, only Liang succeeded in turning a course assignment into a Chinese journal article at the focal university. Notably, this publication did not contribute to her fulfillment of the university's graduation requirements because it was published in a Chinese non-SCI journal. Specifically, one of the courses she took at her home university provided her with an optimal opportunity to participate in Chinese scholarly publishing. The course required students to write an assignment and submit it to an in-house journal for review and publication. The in-house journal was edited by the professor who taught the course and was published by the Nursing Department for an internal readership, i.e., students and faculty members of the School of Medicine as well as practitioners from several hospitals affiliated to the school.[1] A nurturing senior professor who reviewed submissions for the journal was impressed by Liang's article. The professor arranged a meeting with her and encouraged her to submit it to a 'public' in lieu of the in-house journal, which accepted her submission.

Liang spoke highly of that experience, which not only secured a publication for her but also bolstered her confidence in Chinese scholarly publishing. From an activity theory perspective, Liang's course assignment constituted a boundary object and the professor's practice of encouraging her students to submit their assignments to the in-house journal was a boundary practice (Akkerman & Bakker, 2011; Daniels, 2008; Engeström, 1987, 2001, 2010; Engeström et al., 1995; Tuomi-Gröhn et al., 2007). Liang's case indicated potential facilitative roles that boundary objects and

---

[1] The exact number of its affiliated hospitals is not given for the sake of anonymity.

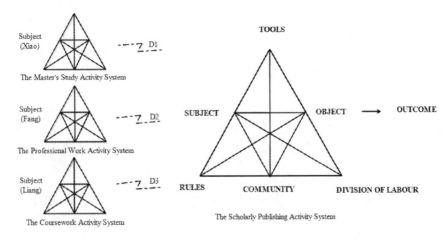

Fig. 4.1 New tensions generated by the adoption of the strategy of starting early

practices could play in doctoral students' scholarly publishing efforts. However, it would come as no surprise that not many doctoral students would have access to boundary practices and mediating resources that Liang had in her endeavour to turn her course assignment into a publication—the chance to submit an assignment to an in-house journal and the encouragement and help of a nurturing professor.

Therefore, despite its popularity and apparent effectiveness, the strategy of starting early proved to be difficult to implement successfully. As the students' accounts revealed, its successful implementation required good preparation or changes in the objects and/or rules of other activity systems, such as the master's study activity system (Xiao), the professional work activity system (Fang), or the coursework activity system (Liang). Figure 4.1 presents schematically the new tensions arising from the adoption of the strategy. Table 4.1 summarises the conditions needed for the successful adoption of the strategy.

As regards the master's study activity system, only Xiao had the opportunity to work on and write up an English manuscript during her master's study. All the other doctoral students in this study and probably many of their fellow students were engaged only in Chinese scholarly publishing during their master's studies, which is common for master's students at universities in Chinese mainland. The university in this study, for example, required its master's students to publish a Chinese journal article before they were allowed to graduate, although the university and supervisors were starting to encourage master's students to publish in English, too (Professor Liu, Interview). The same was true for Xiao's and Cui's alma maters for their master's studies. Moreover, the focal university must be listed as the first affiliation in a publication for it to be counted toward the fulfilment of the university's graduation requirements. Therefore, this strategy would not be practical for students who did their master's studies at another university. In Xiao's case, her first English journal article listed her master's alma mater as her affiliation and hence did not contribute to her fulfillment of the university's publication requirements. Therefore, it would

4.1 Boundary Crossing Through Starting Early

Table 4.1 Changes required for successful boundary crossing through starting early[2]

Case	Changes
The master's study activity system [D1]	• The object shifting from publishing a Chinese journal article to publishing an English journal article • The rules concerning scholarly publishing, particularly affiliation, changing to listing as the first affiliation the university with which students undertake their doctoral rather than master's studies
The professional work activity system [D2]	• The object changing to include publishing English journal articles • Community or workplace being supportive of research and providing access to resources and support from experienced researchers
The coursework activity system [D3]	• The object shifting from mastering of existing knowledge to contributing to knowledge • The rules regarding course assessment changing from formal exams to written assignments

require systemic changes in the object and rules of the master's study activity system to make the strategy work.

Similar changes in the professional activity system would also be needed for the successful employment of Fang's strategy of bringing along manuscripts from her own professional work. As noted above, she benefited from one of her seniors' suggestions about starting early. Additionally, she worked at a prestigious teaching hospital that was affiliated to a medical university and supportive of research. The conducive working environment provided her with access to resources and support from experienced researchers, which made it possible for her to conduct an action research project on nursing education and subsequently turn it into two English manuscripts. However, such resources and support might not be available in other workplaces. For example, Dong, a lecturer at a nursing school affiliated to a top public hospital, pointed out that although she had considered potential research topics for her doctoral thesis and publication before being admitted into the doctoral programme, she was hesitant to start her research because she was concerned about the quality of the work without the guidance and support of a supervisor. As she noted,

> If you start your research completely on your own before your enrolment in a Ph.D. programme, there's no guarantee for the quality of it. Sometimes, you may think you have done a great job. But you might well have neglected some important issues in your project because of your lack of access to guidance, literature, and resources. (Dong, Interview)

With regard to the coursework activity system, the fact that only Liang successfully translated a course assignment into a publication indicated the difficulty in

---

[2] Reprinted from TESOL Quarterly, 53, Jun Lei, Publishing during doctoral candidature from an activity theory perspective: The case of four Chinese nursing doctoral students, Pages 655–684., Copyright (2019), with permission from Wiley.

implementing the strategy. The difficulty might be in part attributable to the focal university's strict assessment guidelines for its various doctoral-level courses, which stipulated that students be assessed primarily through written examinations or a combination of written and oral examinations. Such assessment methods might have prevented the doctoral students from engaging in extensive (English) written assignments, let alone translating them into English scholarly publications. The difficulty might also have to do with the differing objects of the two activity systems. While the object of the coursework activity system was to develop and assess doctoral students' knowledge and skills that were already established and accepted (in Cui's words, 'dead knowledge'), that of the scholarly publishing activity system was to contribute to knowledge and develop doctoral students' knowledge and skills in service to knowledge contribution (Paré, 2010).

Further, Fang suggested that instead of pressurising them to start early, the university should give doctoral students an extra year to publish their Ph.D. research. She believed that the most rigorous way of doing a Ph.D. would be to complete one's Ph.D. project within three years and spend the fourth year writing up and publishing the research results. "In this way," she pointed out, "I write up what I did and what I did is what I want to write about" (Fang, Interview). However, she also admitted that such a change would require "an overhaul" of the doctoral study activity system or a "collective resolution" (Engeström, 1987, cited in Mak & Lee, 2014, p. 83).

To sum up, although the doctoral students valued the strategy of starting early, they had little success with it because its successful enactment demanded changes in the objects and/or rules of other activity systems, such as the master's study activity system, the professional work activity system, or the coursework activity system.

4.2 Refashioning the Scholarly Publishing Activity System

In addition to starting early, another strategy advocated by Professor Liu and adopted by several doctoral students was orchestrating one's own research and publishing activities with those of others. Professor Liu employed the strategy to expedite her students' publishing efforts. Specifically, she divided her research projects among her students so that they could have data to work on as early as possible. As she put it,

> The supervisor must have an overall plan. She must orchestrate all of her research projects and divide them among her students. For example, we have collected a lot of data on the … survivors over the past few years. One of my Ph.D. students [Xiao] managed to publish four SCI journal articles during her candidature and she's grateful that I gave her some data to write on as soon as she was enrolled in the programme.

However, the supervisor needed to strategically manage her research projects to make the orchestrating strategy work, as Professor Liu stated below:

> The supervisor needs to timely comb through the data that her students have collected. For example, I keep a list of all the data I have and I've got a broad idea about how they

could be used to produce various publications. You've got to have such an overview. Then you can ask your students to explore them in depth and see what specific ideas can be derived from the data. Then you can write up articles revolving around those ideas. So a supervisor's orchestrating (of her students' publishing projects) plays a crucial role in her students' success and productivity in publishing. (Professor Liu, Interview)

The above excerpts suggest that supervisors had a vital role to play in the successful implementation of the orchestrating strategy. They also indicate that the strategy was geared toward an overriding concern about the product of scholarly publishing. As illustrated in this and the next sections, such a concern might undermine doctoral students' opportunities for full participation in scholarly publishing. Furthermore, this strategy may also raise ethical concerns. Both Cui and Dong noted that while it might be acceptable for doctoral students to publish papers based on data from their supervisors' research projects, it would be problematic to use data from fellow students' thesis projects. Related to this, Dong pointed out that "similar" collaborative practices might be common in medical research. In particular, she recounted a seminar where a professor from Taiwan shared the secret of his research team's great success in publishing a large number of SCI journal articles. She recalled that according to the professor, his research team had a clear division of labour with groups of researchers respectively tasked to apply for research grants, conduct research, write up research manuscripts, and translate and edit the manuscripts. However, on the interpersonal plane (Rogoff, 1995; Yamagata-Lynch, 2010), the orchestrating strategy differed substantially from the collaborative practice among the researchers in Taiwan. Although they had a clear division of labour in their scholarly publishing activities, it would not be far-fetched to assume that there were close interpersonal coordination and cooperation among them. By contrast, the students who adopted the orchestrating strategy had little or no interpersonal collaboration with those who collected the data and did the foundation work, as some of them probably had already graduated. In this sense, the orchestrating strategy did not involve much collaboration commonly found in the hard disciplines.

Notwithstanding these concerns about the orchestrating strategy, all of the participants acknowledged its effectiveness in helping ameliorate the time pressure for meeting the focal university's publication requirements. Dong, Wei, and Xiao adopted the strategy in their scholarly publishing activities. As noted above, Professor Liu gave Xiao some data to work on while she was still doing her coursework, which, according to Professor Liu, was crucial for her impressive accomplishment of publishing four SCI journal articles during her three-year doctoral candidature. However, her thesis research examined the effectiveness of a care programme for patients with coronary heart disease and was completely unrelated to her published articles. While working on her thesis project—a laboratory medicine project that aimed to improve the treatment of depressive behaviours in animals, Wei published two journal articles about the nursing of trauma survivors to fulfil the university's publication requirements. The data reported in the two journal articles had been collected for one of Professor Liu's research projects. Likewise, working on a doctoral thesis project that investigated the effectiveness of a treatment for patients with depression symptoms, Dong also published an English journal article about the nursing of trauma survivors to fulfil the university's publication requirements. The data for Dong's article also came from one of Professor Liu's (her master's supervisor) research projects. This strategy proved to be effective in helping students to timely meet the university's publication requirements, as in the case of Xiao and Wei, who secured respectively four and two English journal articles during their candidature and graduated on time. Further, although Cui expressed clear disapproval of the strategy in an interview, she changed her mind later on. In a later interview, while still having some reservations about its potential ethical ramifications, she acknowledged its value in ensuring that doctoral students graduate with the degree on time.

Nevertheless, despite its effectiveness in helping students to graduate on time, this strategy failed to assist them in meeting their desire to develop themselves into autonomous knowledge contributors and tended to lead to new tensions. Figure 4.2 depicts new tensions stemming from the adoption of the orchestrating strategy.

First, the orchestrating strategy—a new method for achieving the object of the scholarly publishing activity—changed the division of labour from the subject being involved in all the actions of the activity to only part of the actions. This change triggered a tertiary contradiction (Tension C1 in Fig. 4.2) between the changed division of labour and the object of developing doctoral students into autonomous researchers. Both Fang and Dong were cognizant of this contradiction. Fang, for example, raised concerns about the strategy's potential to sabotage doctoral students' completion of "the (whole) rite of passage" for their doctoral studies (Interview). Dong expressed concerns not only about its potential to undermine doctoral students' opportunities for learning scholarly publishing but also about its possible harm to the development of the nursing discipline: "Doing that [publishing others' research that is not related

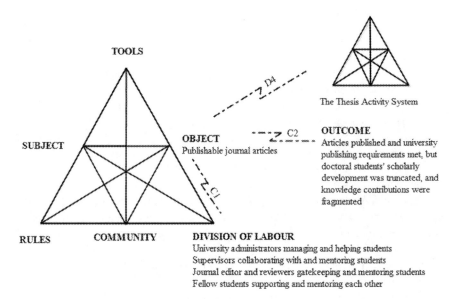

Fig. 4.2 New tensions generated by the adoption of the orchestrating strategy

to one's own thesis research] makes little contribution to the nursing discipline, and it may even obstruct the development of the nursing discipline. Other than getting the degree, it does no good to one's career, either" (Email).

Moreover, the object of the activity system was reformulated as a result of the newly adopted method. Consequently, the activity system was redefined, and the range of actions that the students would be involved in was contracted. Hence, the desired outcome of the scholarly publishing activity was compromised, generating a tension between the activity's object and outcome (Tension C2 in Fig. 4.2). Dong, Fang, and Liang all felt the tension keenly. For instance, Dong's criticism of working on unrelated projects for scholarly publishing and thesis research, which was mentioned above, revealed her concerns about the development of the doctoral students' scholarly abilities and the advancement of the nursing discipline. Liang even thwarted the strategy because of the tension between the redefined and the expected scholarly publishing activity systems, as shown in the following excerpt:

> Now my problem is I haven't finished data collection for my Ph.D. project. So I don't have enough data to write up a manuscript. That's why I haven't written up anything yet. But I have some data that aren't mine but someone else's. I am really torn because some people have written up and published articles drawing upon others' data and allowed other people to use their own data later on. That is kind of a tradition here. But I haven't overcome the barrier yet. So I haven't written up anything based on the data even though I've had them at hand for quite some time. (Interview)

The above excerpt illustrates Liang's dilemma between adopting the orchestrating strategy and publishing her own (thesis) research. Her dilemma lingered on and by the end of her fourth year in the programme, she had not secured an English journal article, the minimal publication requirement for the award of the doctoral degree. Fang also volunteered a similar concern about the misalignment between research and publishing that could arise from the orchestrating strategy, although she did not adopt the strategy herself and was not even prompted in the interviews to discuss it.

> It's impossible to publish an article based on your own Ph.D. project within three years. I know some professors encourage their current students to write and publish on data from their seniors' projects and to leave their own data to their juniors. I'm fine with leaving my data to my juniors and me writing and publishing on my seniors' data. That can speed up our efforts to get our papers published. But it has a drawback. After all, those who did the research know it the best. And I think it would be more systematic to publish your own research, and it would also mean that you've fulfilled the rite of passage (for the doctoral study). (Interview)

For this reason, Fang had a change of heart about the strategy. As she went on to explain:

> I used to approve the strategy. But because the two articles I wrote up drew upon the data I collected while I was working, I feel the whole experiences provided useful guidance for my later research. For example, what I learned about research methodology from those experiences helped me with my thesis project. (Interview)

This excerpt points to learning opportunities that could be afforded by publishing one's thesis research during candidature (see also Kamler, 2008; Mizzi, 2014; Starke-Meyerring, 2011). Meanwhile, Fang's account also alludes to the strategy's potential detrimental ramifications for the thesis research activity system and the development of doctoral students' scholarly abilities.

Indeed, ripple effects from adopting the orchestrating strategy generated a quaternary contradiction between the scholarly publishing activity system and the thesis research activity system (Tension D4 in Fig. 4.2). The activity systems of scholarly publishing and thesis research interacted with each other and were supposed to facilitate each other. However, the adoption of the orchestrating strategy in the former led to a misalignment between its object and that of the latter activity system. The misalignment in turn exerted greater time demands on the students' already stringent schedule. This change of demands might impede students' on-time completion of their thesis research and timely graduation. For example, Dong had to ask for an extension for her thesis project, thus postponing her graduation date. An important reason for her delayed graduation, in her view, was because her thesis project (investigating the effectiveness of a treatment for patients with depression symptoms) was utterly different from the topic of her publication (the health and care of trauma survivors).

Like Dong, both Xiao's and Wei's thesis research projects were completely unrelated to their publications. With the only exception of Fang and Liang who chose their own publication and thesis topics, all the other doctoral students' publication and/or thesis topics were assigned in one way or another by their supervisors. These students were aware and concerned about the misalignment between the two activity systems' objects, as illustrated in the above excerpts. Moreover, according to Xiao, "unlike Western researchers who tend to work on a series of studies centring on one or two themes, Chinese researchers often work on distinctly different research projects" (Interview). She characterised Chinese researchers' practice as "a Chinese characteristic … following whatever is hot in the Western academia" and "having no continuity at all" (Interview).

Professor Liu's rationale for designating the health and care of trauma survivors as her students' publication topics partly confirmed Xiao's observation. Professor Liu believed that the topic was hot and therefore most likely to appeal to the international academic community and that the department had an unmatched advantage to study it because of its expertise and geographical location. As she put it, "there is a gap in the international literature on the topic," and "the topic involves a unique sample [that other researchers do not have easy and ready access to] and has to do with Chinese culture" (Professor Liu, Interview). However, Professor Liu also pointed out that because nursing science is an interdisciplinary discipline and it is extremely difficult to publish in the limited number of high-impact nursing English journals, it is advisable to publish in specialist journals. For this reason, she often advised her students to work on specialist topics for their thesis research, which might stand a better chance of being published in international specialist journals. Notwithstanding Professor Liu's good intentions, the doctoral students expressed concerns that working on totally different projects for their scholarly publishing and thesis research activity systems could diffuse their energy and engagement in each project and thus limit their contributions to knowledge. They seemed to prefer aligning the objects of their scholarly publishing and the thesis research activity systems.

However, aligning scholarly publishing with thesis research was not without problems. Cui, Fang, and Liang attempted to fulfil the university's publication requirements by publishing their own thesis research or research related to their thesis research. Take Fang's case for example. Both her publications and thesis research, as noted above, were concerned with nurse training and education. Her thesis research was built upon two publications growing out of a research project that she conducted during her professional work. Her early start and alignment of her publishing efforts with her thesis research contributed to her on-time graduation.

Both Cui's and Liang's thesis research projects were concerned with the health and care of trauma survivors. However, their projects had different research designs. While Cui's thesis project was a mixed-methods study, Liang's was a longitudinal qualitative study. As both of them noted, Cui's mixed-methods design made it possible for her to collect her quantitative data quickly and thus expedite her publishing efforts. As such, she managed to have an article accepted by an SCI journal three years and five months into her doctoral study. By contrast, Liang lamented that it took her too long to collect her longitudinal qualitative data. Added to this was her unwillingness to resort to the orchestrating strategy. Therefore, while they were enrolled at the same time, Liang had not sent out a manuscript yet by the time Cui secured the publication of her first English article and finished drafting her second one.

The diverging routes and outcomes of these three students' scholarly publishing activities provide further illustrations of the time pressure that the doctoral students were facing to fulfil the university's publication requirements against the competing demands of their doctoral studies. They also point to the importance of orchestrating their scholarly publishing activities if doctoral students are to publish their thesis research or projects related to their thesis research to meet the university's publication requirements.

In sum, although the introduction of the orchestrating strategy into the scholarly publishing activity system alleviated the tension between the object and rules of the scholarly publishing activity system, it generated new contradictions that might undermine the attainment of the object of developing the doctoral students into autonomous researchers who could make knowledge contributions.

4.3 Managerial Roles of the University and Supervisor

Figure 4.3 depicts the tension between the object of developing the doctoral students into autonomous researchers and the overriding roles of the university and supervisors as managers of the doctoral students' timely graduation and prompt publishing of their research (Tension B2).

The tension stemmed from the duality of the object of the scholarly publishing activity system. As will be shown below, it was reflected in the mismatch between the university's and the supervisor's product-oriented support for scholarly publishing on the one hand, and the doctoral students' need for process-oriented support on

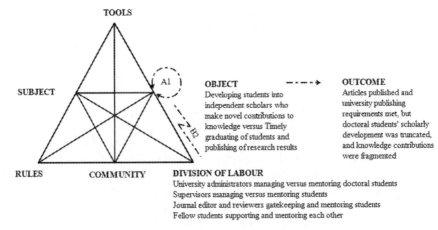

Fig. 4.3 Roles-related tensions concerning scholarly publishing within the doctoral study activity system

the other hand. As discussed in Chap. 3, the university promulgated an array of rules and regulations to structure its doctoral programmes and manage its doctoral students' step-by-step progress toward the completion of their studies. Specifically, the university laid out requirements for the coursework, thesis proposal defence, scholarly publishing, and thesis research. Chapter 3 also made explicit that although these requirements appeared to be concerned with the process of doctoral studies, they were in fact primarily product-oriented. Further, as will be shown below, the support for scholarly publishing provided by the university was "haphazard and unsystematic" (Dong, Interview).

The university's roles

The university's product-oriented approach was most explicit in its publication requirements for its doctoral students. As delineated in Chap. 3, the university, and particularly the School of Medicine, had in place detailed publication requirements for its doctoral students. However, all of the requirements focused primarily on the number and type of journal articles that the doctoral students were expected to publish in order to graduate with degrees. They had no clear guidelines about how they were to achieve the publication requirements (see Li, 2016). They mentioned only in passing possible collaborations with supervisors and with fellow students (sharing credit for articles published in journals with high-impact factors). Even these sections of the requirements focused exclusively on how different types of collaboration would be counted toward the fulfilment of the publication requirements, such as the order of authorship and the impact factors of journals (see Sect. 3.1 for details). Obviously, these requirements reflected the university's principal concern about the outcome rather than the process of collaboration. Similarly, the university had only vague guidelines about how to achieve the object of the thesis research activity system. The only indication was that "the doctoral thesis research should be conducted independently by the doctoral candidate under the guidance of his/her supervisor" (The University Regulations for Doctoral Education). Nor was there any deliberation on the relationship between scholarly publishing and thesis research. The fact that there were many ways to accomplish the objects of the scholarly publishing and thesis research activity systems and to connect them might account for the absence of specific guidelines for how to do so. However, it follows that regardless of the causes for the lack of specific guidelines, such a product-oriented approach was not conducive to doctoral students' successful achievement of the object of developing themselves into autonomous researchers.

Although the university had specific guidelines and regulations about how to achieve the object of the coursework activity system, these guidelines and regulations also reflected its primary concern with the product of doctoral study and scholarly publishing. As a result, the coursework activity system and related activity systems failed to pay sufficient attention to the processes of doctoral students' scholarly publishing. The university, for example, offered no formal academic writing courses. The English academic writing course was conducted as talks, seminars, or workshops. For instance, a cohort completed the course by attending a two-day workshop on writing and publishing SCI journal articles conducted by a former editor of an SCI journal.

As Cui pointed out, although the workshop was useful in familiarising students with the overall procedures of scholarly publishing, it failed to equip them with the specific skills needed for scholarly publishing. She contrasted the workshop with a course on writing English journal articles offered at the partner university. The course was a one-semester course that covered various aspects of writing journal articles, including planning and drafting each section of a journal article, selecting appropriate journals, and submitting, revising, and resubmitting manuscripts. The course required students to complete two written assignments, and the assignments were found to be extremely useful by Cui in improving her scholarly writing abilities. The workshop, by contrast, did not require any such extensive written assignments. For these reasons, Cui concluded that the workshop was "no match to a formal (writing) course" (Cui, interview via QQ).

In addition to workshops, there were talks and seminars on scholarly publishing organised by the university or supervisor and given by either journal editors or published students. Although these talks and seminars were generally deemed useful by the students, four students (i.e., Cui, Dong, Fang, and Xiao) bemoaned that they were held sporadically and unsystematically. As a result, the students rarely communicated with each other formally. As Dong noted,

> Communication among doctoral students is very haphazard and informal. In most cases, if you have something you don't know, you may ask them [your fellow doctoral students]. Likewise, if there's something they don't know, they may ask you, too. That's it. You may learn something accidentally. Rarely do we help each other solve specific problems. (Interview)

Useful as they were, one-shot seminars given by either journal editors or published students were incapable of providing students with process-oriented ongoing support that regular seminars could (see e.g., Lee & Boud, 2003; Lee & Kamler, 2008;

McGrail et al., 2006). Xiao contrasted the lack of regular and formal seminars in the Nursing Department with the weekly seminars organised by her master's supervisor at her master's alma mater, where graduate students could share ideas or "brainstorm" about their research and publishing efforts. Likewise, Fang also mentioned the reading club in the Laboratory Medicine Department, where doctoral students and their supervisors met each week to discuss the latest journal articles, share research ideas, and troubleshoot students' problems with their research and writing.

Furthermore, the students also lamented that the university offered no English editorial services, which could provide ongoing assistance to them during the process of writing. This lack of ongoing writing support at the focal university stood in stark contrast with Xiao's master's alma mater and the partner university. Xiao recalled that her master's alma mater had an English editing services centre that helped faculty and students with their English scholarly publishing. Xiao thought highly of the services provided by the English editing services centre because it played an important role in the successful publishing of her first English journal article. Likewise, the partner university also had such English editorial services, which provided Cui with detailed comments on three drafts of her first English manuscript, and which she found very useful and helpful. Dong and Fang, who were not in the joint-degree programme, learned about the partner university's free English editorial services and hoped that the home university could also provide similar services.

In summary, the doctoral students' accounts in this study indicated a potential role for a formal academic writing course and English editorial services. In addition, it was also shown that the university had no clear guidelines or regulations about supervisors' roles in doctoral students' scholarly publishing efforts. Furthermore, the findings of this study revealed that the doctoral students and their supervisors had differing expectations for the latter's roles in the former's scholarly publishing activities. The supervisors tended to take a product-oriented approach to their students' scholarly publishing activities although it was probably geared toward, as Cui put it, "the greater good" of ensuring students' on-time graduation with the degree. The doctoral students, on the other hand, were inclined to expect process-oriented support for their scholarly publishing efforts. As will be shown below, divergent expectations held by the supervisor and the doctoral students tended to lead to tensions or even conflicts between them.

The supervisor's roles

The doctoral students reported that their supervisors were often too busy to be involved in their scholarly writing processes. As Wei noted, "no one helped me while I was drafting my manuscript. You could only ask others [e.g., your supervisor, your fellow students] to take a look at it after you've finished drafting it" (Interview). Similarly, Dong pointed out that "we have lots of problems with writing and we are on our own to seek assistance. More often than not, we submit our manuscripts to our supervisors only after we've finished drafting them. Only then may they offer us some suggestions. But in reality, we come across many problems in the process of writing" (Interview). In view of this lack of ongoing writing support from the

4.3 Managerial Roles of the University and Supervisor

supervisor, she opined that "it would be great if the supervisor could provide prompt assistance when we encounter problems while writing" (Dong, Interview).

Unlike Dong's overt expression of her desire for more ongoing writing support from the supervisor, Cui and Xiao implicitly expressed their cynical views on the product-oriented approach to scholarly publishing and the general lack of ongoing support for scholarly publishing from the supervisor. When asked to talk about her supervisor's involvement in revising her first English manuscript, Cui remarked that "I think it's OK to ask my supervisor to revise my manuscript because she was very happy when she learned that I'd written up a paper. She knew that she'd be listed as a co-author, so she was willing to revise it" (Interview). Similarly, Xiao said cynically that "basically, you are on your own and you've got to do it by yourself (laughs). Your boss won't bother (to help you). As long as you get your paper published, she'll be happy that she can add one more paper to her publications list" (Text-based interview). These cynical comments are not to be interpreted as personal, because the two students expressed both admiration for and gratitude to their supervisor multiple times in my interviews and interactions with them (see Xiao's account below). Instead, when put into context, their comments appeared to be grievances about the overriding concern with the product of scholarly writing and about the less-than-desirable support that they received in the process of writing.

Cui made her comment when she was drafting her first English manuscript. She later recollected in both her second and third interviews that when she was drafting her first English manuscript, she did not communicate frequently with her supervisor and wished that she had approached and consulted her supervisor earlier and more. Likewise, in Xiao's case, she stated that.

> My supervisor helped me with the ... Journal article (her first English manuscript at the focal university). She helped improve its content and structure. She stayed in ... (an English context) for several years, so her English is very good. She also helped me with the language of my responses to the reviewers' comments. But later on, since I'd published an article with her, she was no longer worried and was more hands-off in my next two articles." (Xiao, Interview)

It is worth noting that Xiao made her cynical comment in a text-based interview on the revision of her third English manuscript written at the focal university. Therefore, her perceived less involvement of her supervisor in her third English manuscript, as she pointed out, might be predicated on her supervisor's confidence in her. Xiao's acutely-felt need for her supervisor's assistance in revising her third English manuscript and her supervisor's confidence in her to do that on her own indicated possible misalignments between supervisor and student expectations for each other. There was, for example, a glaring mismatch between Xiao and her supervisor in their expectations for language support. While Xiao considered her supervisor, Professor Liu, to be "very good" at English and expected to receive language support from her, Professor Liu surprisingly acknowledged that she found it difficult to revise her students' writing and sometimes turned to editorial services for language assistance though she herself had no difficulty writing in English. In Professor Liu's own words, "supervisors have their own limitations. They also need to seek outside help" (Interview).

To summarise, while supervisors were perceived to focus primarily on the product of their doctoral students' scholarly publishing activity system, doctoral students expected their supervisors to play an active role in their processes of scholarly publishing. These varying expectations suggest a need for better communication about expectations between doctoral students and their supervisors. They also point to the need for other sources of help, such as editorial services, in doctoral students' English scholarly publishing endeavours (Lei & Hu, 2015; Li, 2012; Li & Flowerdew, 2007).

4.4 Transformed Practices and Truncated Experiences

This chapter has explored the duality of the object of the scholarly publishing activity system that consisted in developing doctoral students into autonomous researchers while timely graduating them and having their knowledge contributions published. From an activity theory perspective, this is an inner contradiction inherent in doctoral education in today's highly globalised and marketised academy (Aitchison et al., 2012; Delamont et al., 2000; Kamler, 2008; McGrail et al., 2006; Raddon, 2011). Kandiko and Kinchin (2012), for example, characterise "[t]he challenges of a PhD [as] being both a process of learning (for the student and the supervisor) and a product of a research project" (p. 3). Moreover, primary contradictions in activity systems cannot be resolved completely (Cole & Engeström, 1993; Engeström, 1987, 1999, 2001; Engeström & Miettinen, 1999; Roth & Lee, 2007). As a result, despite the doctoral students' attempts to tackle the object-rules-related and the object-roles-related secondary contradictions, the primary contradiction remained unresolved, as reflected in the new tensions arising from the doctoral students' efforts to address those secondary contradictions.

Specifically, the object-rules-related contradiction lay in attaining the object of scholarly publishing while meeting the competing demands of the doctoral study activity system within a tight timeframe. The contradiction was most notably reflected in the time pressure that all of the six students reported encountering in their scholarly publishing activity systems. The time pressure arose from the doctoral students' simultaneous engagement in multiple, and often competing, activity systems within their doctoral studies, including coursework, scholarly publishing, and thesis research, among others (Beauchamp et al., 2009; Casanave, 2010; Lundell & Beach, 2003; Prior, 1998; Prior & Min, 2008; Simpson, 2013; Vekkaila et al., 2012). These activity systems placed onerous demands upon the doctoral students and competed against each other for their limited time. McAlpine and McKinnon (2013) also found that the doctoral students in their study had to "handl[e] competing claims on their time" on a daily basis (p. 278). Regarding the tensions between thesis and publishing, Mizzi (2014) pointed out that "doctoral students may feel incapable of balancing out the workload among dissertations and other publications" (p. 55). These challenges suggest the importance of carefully

4.4 Transformed Practices and Truncated Experiences

planning and managing scholarly publishing, and particularly aligning it with other activities in successful scholarly publishing during doctoral candidature.

To cope with the time pressure, the doctoral students resorted to the strategies of starting early and orchestrating their own research and publishing activities with those of others, which, while ameliorating the tension to some extent, led to new contradictions. To begin, the strategy of starting early was highly valued by all of the participants. Their valorisation of the strategy is not surprising considering that starting writing (i.e., thesis and publications) early is a strategy widely recommended for doctoral students in the literature (e.g., Delamont et al., 2000; Golde, 2005; Hartley & Betts, 2009; Kamler, 2008; Kiley, 2011). Aitchison et al. (2012), for example, observe that "doctoral students are expected to be, or to quickly become, proficient and prolific writers" of both thesis and publication (p. 435). The doctoral students in the present study started early by bringing data or manuscripts from the professional work activity system (Fang) or the master's study activity system (Xiao), or by turning a course assignment into a publication (Liang).

From an activity theory perspective, the strategy of starting early hinges on the outcomes of an earlier activity system that functions as tools or boundary objects for the scholarly publishing activity system (Casanave, 2010; Lundell & Beach, 2003; see also Barab et al., 2002; Hasu & Engeström, 2000; Miettinen, 2005). Likewise, it is a practice of boundary crossing to link other activity systems with the scholarly publishing activity system (Beauchamp et al., 2009; Y. Li, 2014; Lundell & Beach, 2003; see also Akkerman & Bakker, 2011; Daniels, 2008; Engeström, 2010; Engeström et al., 1995; Tuomi-Gröhn & Engeström, 2007; Tuomi-Gröhn et al., 2007). However, because different activity systems have different objects, rules, and division of labour, linking them successfully requires aligning the objects and/or rules of the scholarly publishing activity system with those of other activity systems. The cases of Fang, Liang, and Xiao showed that it is difficult to make such connections or cross the boundaries between the scholarly publishing activity system and the other three activity systems.

Take, for example, Liang's strategy of turning a course assignment into a Chinese publication, a strategy that has also been documented in the literature (e.g., Casanave, 2010; Lee & Norton, 2003; Lundell & Beach, 2003; Matsuda, 2003; Mizzi, 2014). As noted above, Liang's case exemplified an optimal scenario, where the objects of the coursework assignment and the scholarly publishing activity systems were aligned through a boundary object and a boundary practice (Akkerman & Bakker, 2011; Daniels, 2008; Engeström, 1987, 2001, 2010; Engeström et al., 1995; Tuomi-Gröhn et al., 2007). Casanave (2010) reported similar "intermediate practices, between class work and the professional activity of publishing" (p. 55), where with the help of a faculty member, graduate students edited a series of papers on particular topics, colloquia proceedings, and working papers from course assignments. As Casanave (2010) pointed out, these practices can help students "make connections among class work, dissertations, and future publications rather than see their work as fragmented and unrelated to dissertation and publication" (p. 55). The examples in Casanave's study and Liang's case in this study indicate that boundary objects and practices have the potential to facilitate doctoral students' scholarly publishing activities. However, it should also be noted that not many doctoral students would have access to boundary practices and mediating resources that the students in Casanave's study and Liang in the present study had in their attempts to cross the boundaries between the coursework and scholarly publishing activity systems. Similarly, successfully crossing the boundaries between the professional work and the scholarly publishing activity system (Fang) or between the master's study and the scholarly publishing activity system (Xiao) would also require changes in the objects and/or rules of the activity systems involved.

Furthermore, the study revealed potential challenges in making connections between thesis research and scholarly publishing. This finding adds further evidence to the literature (Hartley & Betts, 2009; Kamler, 2008; Lee, 2010; Lee & Aitchison, 2011; Lee & Kamler, 2008; Lundell & Beach, 2003; Robins & Kanowski, 2008; Simpson, 2013), which has documented the difficulty of transforming theses into publications. Simpson (2013), for example, refers to the difficulty as "a systematic conflict" (p. 243). Similarly, Lundell and Beach (2003) label it as "a double bind arising from the contradiction between writing according to the genre rules of the Graduate School and department systems and writing for publications and conference papers" (p. 503). To successfully transform theses into publications requires recontextualising the former in terms of genre conventions, audience, and so on (Lee & Kamler, 2008; Lundell & Beach, 2003; Simpson, 2013).

Likewise, writing article-compilation theses also entails recontextualising. In addition, writing a compilation thesis demands strategic planning and management of thesis and manuscript writing (Kwan, 2010, 2013; Lee & Aitchison, 2011), including designing and developing publications that have an adequate scope for a doctoral thesis and making the parts a coherent whole. Lee and Aitchison (2011), for example, observe that "for students under pressure to complete their doctoral studies in a timely fashion and produce a dissertation as well as publications en route, there are very real challenges concerning how to manage writing multiple related texts" (p. 69). In this regard, Kwan (2010) suggests "produc[ing] a thesis following the article compilation (AC) format" (p. 59) by aligning the activities of conducting research, writing up the thesis, and publishing. Likewise, Casanave (2010) recommends "dovetailing" activity systems of class work, thesis, and scholarly publishing to make connections among them and to avoid "duplica[ting] (efforts and resources) needlessly" (p. 55). These findings suggest that it is difficult to cross boundaries between different activity systems.

Unlike the strategy of starting early that has been widely documented in the literature, the strategy of orchestrating one's own research and publishing with those of others has received relatively little attention.[3] Although it appeared to be an example of collaboration commonly found in the hard disciplines (Becher & Trowler, 2001; Brew et al., 2011; Delamont et al., 2000; Hakala, 2009), it was not real collaboration. The strategy seemed to be related to both the interdisciplinary nature of the nursing

---

[3] But Li and Flowerdew (2007) and Cargill et al. (2012) have reported a different but related practice, where supervisors or post-doctoral fellows write up papers based on data collected by Ph.D. students and assign first authorship to the latter to help them graduate on time.

4.4 Transformed Practices and Truncated Experiences

science and the supervisor's perceived effectiveness of the strategy in fostering her students' scholarly publishing efforts. Five of the six doctoral students' publications (except Fang) centred on the health and care of trauma survivors and appeared to partly follow the hard science tradition, where doctoral students work as a research team under the supervision of one or several supervisors, are assigned research topics related to a larger research project, and where senior students also shoulder the supervisory responsibility (Delamont et al., 2000; Hakala, 2009; Kandiko & Kinchin, 2012; Lee & Aitchison, 2011; Watts, 2012; Yates, 2010). Delamont et al. (2000) classify this mode of doctoral education or socialisation as the "position mode." It seems that the nursing discipline or the Nursing Department was tilting towards the position mode probably due to the pressure on doctoral students to publish during candidature, a trend that has also been observed in some typical humanities and social sciences (Hakala, 2009; Lee & Kamler, 2008; Parry, 2007).

Conversely, their thesis research projects varied widely because Professor Liu considered it advisable to work on specialist topics, given the limited number of high-impact English nursing journals and the difficulty of getting published in them. Thus, the students' thesis research projects appeared to follow the humanities and social science tradition or what Delamont et al. (2000) refer to as the "personal mode," where students develop their own research topics, work on their own, have no research teams to support them, and have a more personal relationship with their supervisors. As a whole, therefore, faced with the pressure to meet the university's publication requirements in a timely fashion within their busy doctoral studies, the doctoral students and their supervisors generated their "subcultural responses" to "get by" (Delamont et al., 2000, p. 10). In this sense, a subculture of scholarly publishing and thesis research was in the making in the Nursing Department. In such a subculture, as pointed out by Cui and Dong and alluded to by Liang, what kinds of and how much collaboration among fellow students are acceptable for scholarly publishing and thesis research, and what kinds of organisational structures are most appropriate for this emerging subculture are issues worthy of further research (see also Simpson, 2013).

Also related to the orchestrating strategy was whether and to what extent it was supervisors' responsibility to help their doctoral students to meet the institutional publication requirements. In this regard, extant research has found that while some supervisors take it upon themselves to help their doctoral students to publish their research, others do not consider it to be their job (Aitchison et al., 2012; Li, 2016). As pointed out in Chap. 3 and alluded to in this chapter, on-time graduation with the degree appeared to be the top priority for both the supervisor and the students themselves, "the greater good", as Cui put it. Professor Liu viewed it as an important part of her responsibilities as a supervisor and took great pride in the timely graduation of her students. This view differs sharply from that of a professor in Li's (2016) study, who did not think that "supervisors are responsible for their students' meeting of the publication requirement" (p. 5) and who believed that "[students] should write on their own" (p. 5), though he himself did help his students revise their papers. Li also recounted a news story on the Science Net (*kexuewang*, a portal for Chinese scientists, www.sciencenet.cn) about another professor, who deferred submitting for publication the works of his doctoral students, resulting in their failures to meet the publication requirements and obtain their doctoral degrees. As Li noted, the online community expressed sympathy toward the students and raised questions about the supervisor's ability and integrity. Therefore, with the high-stakes mandate of "publishing SCI journal articles or no degree," whether and to what extent supervisors should be involved in their students' scholarly publishing efforts to meet the institutional publication requirement is also an interesting and important issue meriting further research.

Furthermore, unlike the new tensions emanating from the strategy of starting early that called for changes in the objects and/or rules of other activity systems, the new tensions stemming from the orchestrating strategy led to a contraction of learning possibilities for the doctoral students and a changed scholarly publishing activity system. Specifically, in order to help her students attain the product aspect of the object of their doctoral studies—i.e., meeting the university's publication requirements and graduating on time with the degree, Professor Liu orchestrated their scholarly publishing and thesis research activities and, in the process, dynamically reconstructed the objects of the activity systems involved (Engeström, 1987; Kaptelinin, 2005). As a result, the strategy triggered changes in the rules and/or division of labour in the scholarly publishing activity system. These changes reshaped the major stakeholders' actions accordingly, which not only truncated the doctoral students' engagement in the actions of scholarly publishing and thus fragmented their learning experiences and opportunities, but also reinforced the overriding product-oriented object and further undermined the attainment of the process-oriented object. This is similar to the case of some students in Barab et al.'s (2002) study, who participated in only part of the actions of learning astronomy using 3-D modelling and thus acquired only partial knowledge about it. Such contractions of opportunities for learning to write for publication have also been documented in the literature. Drawing upon her own study (Li, 2012) and Blakeslee's (1997) study, Li (2016) points out that novice researchers' learning to write for publication might be undercut when senior researchers take over part of the actions due to the pressure to publish in high-impact journals or to meet the deadline (see also Huang, 2010).

The object-roles-related contradiction concerned the tension between the object of developing the doctoral students into autonomous researchers and the university and supervisor's principal roles as managers of the product of the doctoral students' scholarly publishing activities. This contradiction was mainly reflected in differing expectations for whether and what types of support the university and supervisor should provide for the doctoral students' scholarly publishing activities, i.e., managerial or mentoring. Bonneau (2013) notes that the primary contradiction in various fields and disciplines is characterised in the literature "as an opposition between 'managerial logic' and 'professional logic'" (p. 9, see also Hughes & Tight, 2013; Lundell & Beach, 2003). As is the case with many fields, the higher education sector has witnessed a growing dominance of the "managerial logic" (i.e., managing and auditing the outcomes of doctoral education, such as the number of graduates and publications) over the "professional logic" (i.e., reproducing knowledge producers and producing knowledge), as evidenced in the shift of focus away from the process to the product of doctoral education (Can & Walker, 2014; Kandiko & Kinchin, 2012; Lee & Aitchison, 2011; McCormack, 2004; Paré, 2010; Raddon, 2011; Starke-Meyerring et al., 2014). McCormack (2004), for example, found in her study that the focal "institution's conception of research as a commodity undertaken in an economic/market-oriented context focused on speedy completion and measurable outcomes" (p. 323).

As regards institutional support, the findings of this study revealed that although the university mandated regulations and events or activities (e.g., workshops, seminars, and talks) to support doctoral students' scholarly publishing efforts, it paid insufficient attention to their processes of scholarly writing and publishing. Although the various regulations and requirements instituted by the university appeared to be concerned with the process of doctoral studies, they were in fact preoccupied with the product and outcome at the expense of the process and experience of learning (see also McCormack, 2004; Paré, 2010; Raddon, 2011). The workshops, seminars, and talks offered at the university constituted what Lee and Kamler (2008) call "'masterclass,' where facilitators are typically published writers, significant figures in the field, journal editors and publishers" (p. 512). "While clearly valuable," as they point out, "this kind of pedagogical work is generally sporadic and mostly ad hoc, rather than sustained or part of a broader reconceptualisation of doctoral education" (Lee & Kamler, 2008, p. 512). Moreover, in a review of the effectiveness of three types of interventions (i.e., writing support groups, writing courses, and provision of a writing coach or formal mentor) in increasing academic staff's publication output, McGrail et al. (2006) found sporadic and short-term didactic writing courses to be "the least beneficial in terms of an immediate return of published papers" (p. 34). Based on their review, McGrail et al. (2006) conclude that "[a] regular, ongoing arrangement seems to be most beneficial" (p. 34). Similarly, Lee and Kamler (2008) note that "[r]ecent research … confirms the importance of direct, ongoing support in increasing publication from doctoral inquiry" (p. 512, see also Lee & Boud, 2003).

Therefore, the findings of this study indicate that the university might not be aware of what support and resources are needed by doctoral students to publish successfully (Aitchison et al., 2010b; Curry & Lillis, 2013). As Aitchison et al.'s (2010a) observe, "universities are … often not skillful in recognizing the pedagogical work involved in bringing students into a productive relationship with the practices of publication" (p. 3). These findings suggest a need for universities to provide doctoral students with ongoing progress-oriented support (e.g., a formal academic writing course and English editorial services) and to better understand how to provide the support most effectively. This resonates with recent calls in the literature for pedagogy on scholarly publishing (Aitchison et al., 2010a; Cotterall, 2011; Kwan, 2010, 2013; Lee & Kamler, 2008; Li, 2016; Li & Flowerdew, 2007; Morss & Murray, 2001).

Similarly, regarding supervisory support, the findings of this study found different expectations held by the supervisors and the doctoral students for the former's roles in the latter's scholarly publishing efforts. The most salient difference lay in the professors' outcome-oriented approach to their doctoral students' scholarly publishing activities and the doctoral students' expectations for ongoing process-oriented support from their supervisors, as aptly captured by Cui's and Xiao's cynical views on their supervisor's outcome-oriented approach to their scholarly publishing endeavours. This difference might have to do with their varying valorisation of the outcome- and process-oriented motives for scholarly publishing. In addition, this study also revealed that the supervisor seemed to have limited ability to provide language support although she did not have difficulty writing in English herself. Previous research has also documented supervisors' restricted ability to provide certain types of assistance (e.g., language support) in scholarly publishing (Bazerman, 2009; Kwan, 2010, 2013; Lei & Hu, 2015; Li & Flowerdew, 2007; Paré, 2010; Strauss et al., 2003). As Paré et al. (2011) point out, while supervisors may have no difficulty performing "the knowledge-making practices of their research communities" (p. 223), such as "the implicit (and tacit) regularities and routines of the discipline" (p. 217), they may have problems articulating them. Surprisingly, in contrast to the supervisor's acknowledgement of her limited ability to help her students with their language problems, her students believed that she is very good at English academic writing and should therefore have no problem providing them with language assistance. Such divergent views underline possible mismatches in expectations about supervisors' roles in their students' scholarly publishing activities. These findings point to the need for better communication between supervisors and their students and for other sources of help if doctoral students are to publish successfully during their candidature.

4.5 Conclusion

This chapter has looked into the object-related contradiction concerning the doctoral students' scholarly publishing practices within their busy doctoral studies. The findings have revealed that as an inherent contradiction within the scholarly publishing activity system, this object-related primary contradiction was manifested in the object-rules and the object-roles secondary contradictions. The object-rules and the object-roles secondary contradictions were in turn reflected mainly in the time pressure faced by the doctoral students in meeting the university's publication requirements and in the less-than-desirable product-oriented support from the university and supervisor, respectively. The findings have also indicated that while the doctoral students were able to ameliorate some of the difficulties and challenges related to the secondary contradictions, the primary contradiction remained unresolved. The reason for this has to do with the nature of the contradiction as an inherent contradiction. The difficulty or impossibility of resolving the primary contradiction was manifested in the fact that attempts to address the secondary contradictions led to new contradictions. These findings suggest the need to bring in other sources of help and to better interweave or cross boundaries between different activity systems.

As will be illustrated in the next chapter, the doctoral students in this study resorted to an array of additional resources to mediate their scholarly publishing efforts. As the pressure to publish is likely to increase rather than abate, the tension between the product and process of scholarly publishing may well exacerbate. It should however be noted that the product- and process-oriented approaches are not to be taken as dichotomous but dialectical. Therefore, interweaving process-oriented and product-oriented actions and practices may prove to be a practical way to ameliorate the tension between them and thereby enrich doctoral students' learning experiences.

References

Aitchison, C., Catterall, J., Ross, P., & Burgin, S. (2012). 'Tough love and tears': Learning doctoral writing in the sciences. *Higher Education Research & Development, 31*, 435–447. https://doi.org/10.1080/07294360.2011.559195

Aitchison, C., Kamler, B., & Lee, A. (2010a). Introduction: Why publishing pedagogies? In C. Aitchison, B. Kamler, & A. Lee (Eds.), *Publishing pedagogies for the doctorate and beyond* (pp. 1–11). Routledge.

Aitchison, C., Kamler, B., & Lee, A. (2010b). *Publishing pedagogies for the doctorate and beyond*. Routledge.

Akkerman, S. F., & Bakker, A. (2011). Boundary crossing and boundary objects. *Review of Educational Research, 81*, 132–169. https://doi.org/10.3102/0034654311404435

Barab, S. A., Barnett, M., & Yamagata-Lynch, L., Squire, K., & Keating, T. (2002). Using activity theory to understand the systemic tensions characterizing a technology-rich introductory astronomy course. *Mind, Culture, and Activity, 9*, 76–107. https://doi.org/10.1207/s15327884mca0902_02

Bazerman, C. (2009). Genre and cognitive development: Beyond writing to learn. In C. Bazerman, A. Bonin, & D. Figueiredo (Eds.), *Genre in a changing world* (pp. 279–294). The WAC Clearinghouse.

Beauchamp, C., Jazvac-Martek, M., & McAlpine, L. (2009). Studying doctoral education: Using activity theory to shape methodological tools. *Innovations in Education and Teaching International, 46*, 265–277. https://doi.org/10.1080/14703290903068839

Becher, T., & Trowler, P. R. (2001). *Academic tribes and territories: Intellectual enquiry and the culture of disciplines* (2nd ed.). Open University Press.

Blakeslee, A. M. (1997). Activity, context, interaction, and authority. *Journal of Business and Technical Communication, 11*, 125–169. https://doi.org/10.1177/1050651997011002001

Bonneau, C. (2013, July 4–6). *Contradictions and their concrete manifestations: An activity-theoretical analysis of the intra-organizational co-configuration of open source software*. The 29th EGOS Colloquium, Montréal, Canada.

Brew, A., Boud, D., & Un Namgung, S. (2011). Influences on the formation of academics: The role of the doctorate and structured development opportunities. *Studies in Continuing Education, 33*, 51–66. https://doi.org/10.1080/0158037x.2010.515575

Can, G., & Walker, A. (2014). Social science doctoral students' needs and preferences for written feedback. *Higher Education, 68*, 303–318. https://doi.org/10.1007/s10734-014-9713-5

Cargill, M., O'Connor, P., & Li, Y. (2012). Educating Chinese scientists to write for international journals: Addressing the divide between science and technology education and English language teaching. *English for Specific Purposes, 31*, 60–69. https://doi.org/10.1016/j.esp.2011.05.003

Casanave, C. P. (2010). Dovetailing under impossible circumstances. In C. Aitchison, B. Kamler, & A. Lee (Eds.), *Publishing pedagogies for the doctorate and beyond* (pp. 47–63). Routledge.

Cole, M., & Engeström, Y. (1993). A cultural-historical approach to distributed cognition. In G. Salomon (Ed.), *Distributed cognitions: Psychological and educational considerations* (pp. 1–46). Cambridge University Press.

Cotterall, S. (2011). Doctoral students writing: Where's the pedagogy? *Teaching in Higher Education, 16*, 413–425. https://doi.org/10.1080/13562517.2011.560381

Curry, M. J., & Lillis, T. (2013). Introduction to the thematic issue: Participating in academic publishing—consequences of linguistic policies and practices. *Language Policy, 12*, 209–213. https://doi.org/10.1007/s10993-013-9286-7

Daniels, H. (2008). *Vygotsky and research*. Routledge.

Delamont, S., Atkinson, P., & Parry, O. (2000). *The doctoral experience: Success and failure in graduate school*. Falmer Press.

Engeström, Y. (1987). *Learning by expanding: An activity-theoretical approach to developmental research*. Orienta-Konsultit.

Engeström, Y. (1999). Activity theory and individual and social transformation. In Y. Engeström, R. Miettinen, & R. Punamäki (Eds.), *Perspectives on activity theory* (pp. 19–38). Cambridge University Press.

Engeström, Y. (2001). Expansive learning at work: Toward an activity theoretical reconceptualization. *Journal of Education and Work, 14*, 133–156.

Engeström, Y. (2010). Activity theory and learning at work. In M. Malloch, L. Cairns, K. Evans, & B. N. O'Connor (Eds.), *The Sage handbook of workplace learning* (pp. 74–89). Sage.

Engeström, Y., Engeström, R., & Kärkkäinen, M. (1995). Polycontextuality and boundary crossing in expert cognition: Learning and problem solving in complex work activities. *Learning and Instruction, 5*, 319–336. https://doi.org/10.1016/0959-4752(95)00021-6

Engeström, Y., & Miettinen, R. (1999). Introduction. In Y. Engeström, R. Miettinen, & R. Punamäki (Eds.), *Perspectives on activity theory* (pp. 1–16). Cambridge University Press.

Golde, C. M. (2005). The role of the department and discipline in doctoral student attrition: Lessons from four departments. *Journal of Higher Education, 76*, 669–700. https://doi.org/10.1353/jhe.2005.0039

Hakala, J. (2009). Socialization of junior researchers in new academic research environments: Two case studies from Finland. *Studies in Higher Education, 34*, 501–516. https://doi.org/10.1080/03075070802597119

Hartley, J., & Betts, L. (2009). Publishing before the thesis: 58 postgraduate views. *Higher Education Review, 41*, 29–44.

Hasu, M., & Engeström, Y. (2000). Measurement in action: An activity-theoretical perspective on producer–user interaction. *International Journal of Human-Computer Studies, 53*, 61–89. https://doi.org/10.1006/ijhc.2000.0375

Huang, J. C. (2010). Publishing and learning writing for publication in English: Perspectives of NNES PhD students in science. *Journal of English for Academic Purposes, 9*, 33–44. https://doi.org/10.1016/j.jeap.2009.10.001

Hughes, C., & Tight, M. (2013). The metaphors we study by: The doctorate as a journey and/or as work. *Higher Education Research & Development, 32*, 765–775. https://doi.org/10.1080/07294360.2013.777031

Kamler, B. (2008). Rethinking doctoral publication practices: Writing from and beyond the thesis. *Studies in Higher Education, 33*, 283–294. https://doi.org/10.1080/03075070802049236

Kandiko, C. B., & Kinchin, I. M. (2012). What is a doctorate? A concept-mapped analysis of process versus product in the supervision of lab-based PhDs. *Educational Research, 54*, 3–16. https://doi.org/10.1080/00131881.2012.658196

Kaptelinin, V. (2005). The object of activity: Making sense of the sense-maker. *Mind, Culture, and Activity, 12*, 4–18. https://doi.org/10.1207/s15327884mca1201_2

Kiley, M. (2011). Developments in research supervisor training: Causes and responses. *Studies in Higher Education, 36*, 585–599. https://doi.org/10.1080/03075079.2011.594595

Kwan, B. S. C. (2010). An investigation of instruction in research publishing offered in doctoral programs: The Hong Kong case. *Higher Education, 59*, 55–68. https://doi.org/10.1007/s10734-009-9233-x

Kwan, B. S. C. (2013). Facilitating novice researchers in project publishing during the doctoral years and beyond: A Hong Kong-based study. *Studies in Higher Education, 38*, 207–225. https://doi.org/10.1080/03075079.2011.576755

Lee, A. (2010). When the aticle is the dissertation: Pedagogies for a PhD by publication. In C. Aitchison, B. Kamler, & A. Lee (Eds.), *Publishing pedagogies for the doctorate and beyond* (pp. 12–29). Routledge.

Lee, A., & Aitchison, C. (2011). Working with tensions: Writing for publication during your doctorate. In T. S. Rocco & T. Hatcher (Eds.), *The handbook of scholarly writing and publishing* (pp. 62–74). Jossey Bass.

Lee, A., & Boud, D. (2003). Writing groups, change and academic identity: Research development as local practice. *Studies in Higher Education, 28*, 187–200. https://doi.org/10.1080/0307507032000058109

Lee, A., & Kamler, B. (2008). Bringing pedagogy to doctoral publishing. *Teaching in Higher Education, 13*, 511–523. https://doi.org/10.1080/13562510802334723

Lee, E., & Norton, B. (2003). Demystifying publishing: A collaborative exchange between graduate student and supervisor. In C. P. Casanave & S. Vandrick (Eds.), *Writing for scholarly publication: Behind the scenes in language education* (pp. 17–38). Lawrence Erlbaum.

Lei, J., & Hu, G. (2015). Apprenticeship in scholarly publishing: A student perspective on doctoral supervisors' roles. *Publications, 3*, 27–42. https://doi.org/10.3390/publications3010027

Li, Y. (2012). "I have no time to find out where the sentences came from; I just rebuild them": A biochemistry professor eliminating novices' textual borrowing. *Journal of Second Language Writing, 21*, 59–70. https://doi.org/10.1016/j.jslw.2012.01.001

Li, Y. (2014). Boundary crossing: Chinese orthopedic surgeons as researchers. *Journal of Technical Writing and Communication, 44*, 423–449. https://doi.org/10.2190/TW.44.4.e

Li, Y. (2016). "Publish SCI papers or no degree": Practices of Chinese doctoral supervisors in response to the publication pressure on science students. *Asia Pacific Journal of Education, 36*, 545–558. https://doi.org/10.1080/02188791.2015.1005050

Li, Y., & Flowerdew, J. (2007). Shaping Chinese novice scientists' manuscripts for publication. *Journal of Second Language Writing, 16*, 100–117. https://doi.org/10.1016/j.jslw.2007.05.001

Lundell, D. B., & Beach, R. (2003). Dissertation writers' negotiations with competing activity systems. In C. Bazerman & D. Russell (Eds.), *Writing selves/writing societies* (pp. 483–514). The WAC Clearinghouse.

Mak, P., & Lee, I. (2014). Implementing assessment for learning in L2 writing: An activity theory perspective. *System, 47*, 73–87. https://doi.org/10.1016/j.system.2014.09.018

Matsuda, P. K. (2003). Coming to voice: Publishing as a graduate student. In C. P. Casanave & S. Vandrick (Eds.), *Writing for scholarly publication: Behind the scenes in language education* (pp. 39–51). Lawrence Erlbaum.

McAlpine, L., & McKinnon, M. (2013). Supervision—the most variable of variables: Student perspectives. *Studies in Continuing Education, 35*, 265–280. https://doi.org/10.1080/0158037x.2012.746227

McCormack, C. (2004). Tensions between student and institutional conceptions of postgraduate research. *Studies in Higher Education, 29*, 319–334. https://doi.org/10.1080/0307507042000168260

McGrail, M. R., Rickard, C. M., & Jones, R. (2006). Publish or perish: A systematic review of interventions to increase academic publication rates. *Higher Education Research & Development, 25*, 19–35. https://doi.org/10.1080/07294360500453053

Miettinen, R. (2005). Object of activity and individual motivation. *Mind, Culture, and Activity, 12*, 52–69. https://doi.org/10.1207/s15327884mca1201_5

Mizzi, R. C. (2014). Writing realities: An exploration of drawbacks and benefits of publishing while enrolled in a doctoral program. *New Horizons in Adult Education and Human Resource Development, 26*, 54–59. https://doi.org/10.1002/nha3.20063

Morss, K., & Murray, R. (2001). Researching academic writing within a structured programme: Insights and outcomes. *Studies in Higher Education, 26*, 35–52. https://doi.org/10.1080/030750 70020030706

Paré, A. (2010). Slow the presses: Concerns for premature publication. In C. Aitchison, B. Kamler, & A. Lee (Eds.), *Publishing pedagogies for the doctorate and beyond* (pp. 30–46). Routledge.

Paré, A., Starke-Meyerring, D., & McAlpine, L. (2011). Knowledge and identity work in the supervision of doctoral student writing: Shaping rhetorical subjects. In D. Starke-Meyerring, A. Paré, N. Artemeva, M. Horne, & L. Yousoubova (Eds.), *Writing in knowledge societies* (pp. 215–236). Parlor Press and WAC Clearinghouse.

Parry, S. (2007). *Disciplines and doctorates: Higher education dynamics*. Springer.

Prior, P. (1998). *Writing/disciplinarity: A sociohistoric account of literate activity in the academy*. Lawrence Erlbaum.

Prior, P., & Min, Y. K. (2008). The lived experience of graduate work and writing: From chronotopic laminations to everyday lamentations. In C. P. Casanave & X. Li (Eds.), *Learning the literate practices of graduate school: Insiders' reflections on academic enculturation* (pp. 230–246). University of Michigan Press.

Raddon, A. E. (2011). A changing environment: Narratives of learning about research. *International Journal for Researcher Development, 2*, 26–45. https://doi.org/10.1108/17597511111178005

Robins, L., & Kanowski, P. (2008). PhD by publication: A student's perspective. *Journal of Research Practice, 4*(2), M3. http://jrp.icaap.org/index.php/jrp/article/view/136/154

Rogoff, B. (1995). Observing sociocultural activity on three planes: Participatory appropriation, guided participation, and apprenticeship. In J. V. Wertsch, P. del Rio, & A. Alvarez (Eds.), *Sociocultural studies of mind* (pp. 139–164). Cambridge University Press.

Roth, W.-M., & Lee, Y.-J. (2007). "Vygotsky's neglected legacy": Cultural-historical activity theory. *Review of Educational Research, 77*, 186–232. https://doi.org/10.3102/0034654306298273

Simpson, S. (2013). Systems of writing response: A Brazilian student's experiences writing for publication in an environmental sciences doctoral program. *Research in the Teaching of English, 48*, 228–249.

Starke-Meyerring, D. (2011). The paradox of writing in doctoral education: Student experiences. In L. McAlpine & C. Amundsen (Eds.), *Doctoral education: Research-based strategies for doctoral students, supervisors and administrators* (pp. 75–95). Springer.

Starke-Meyerring, D., Paré, A., Sun, K. Y., & El-Bezre, N. (2014). Probing normalized institutional discourses about writing: The case of the doctoral thesis. *Journal of Academic Language and Learning, 8*, 13–27.

Strauss, P., Walton, J. A., & Madsen, S. (2003). "I don't have time to be an English teacher": Supervising the EAL thesis. *Hong Kong Journal of Applied Linguistics, 8*, 1–16.

Tuomi-Gröhn, T., & Engeström, Y. (2007). Conceptualizing transfer: From standard notions to developmental perspectives. In T. Tuomi-Gröhn & Y. Engeström (Eds.), *Between school and work: New perspectives on transfer and boundary crossing* (pp. 19–38). Emerald.

Tuomi-Gröhn, T., Engeström, Y., & Young, M. (2007). From transfer to boundary-crossing between school and work as a tool for developing vocational education: An introduction. In T. Tuomi-Gröhn & Y. Engeström (Eds.), *Between school and work: New perspectives on transfer and boundary crossing* (pp. 1–15). Emerald.

Vekkaila, J., Pyhältö, K., Hakkarainen, K., Keskinen, J., & Lonka, K. (2012). Doctoral students' key learning experiences in the natural sciences. *International Journal for Researcher Development, 3*, 154–183. https://doi.org/10.1108/17597511311316991

Watts, J. H. (2012). To publish or not to publish before submission? Considerations for doctoral students and supervisors. *Creative Education, 3*, 1101–1107. https://doi.org/10.4236/ce.2012.326165

Yamagata-Lynch, L. C. (2010). *Activity systems analysis methods: Understanding complex learning environments*. Springer.

Yates, L. (2010). Quality agendas and doctoral work: The tacit, the new agendas, the changing contexts. In P. Thomson & M. Walker (Eds.), *The Routledge doctoral student's companion* (pp. 299–310). Routledge.

Chapter 5
Doctoral Students' Dual Identities: Constraints and Affordances of Doctoral Publication

Chapter 4 has examined the object-related contradiction—the duality of the object of developing the doctoral students into autonomous researchers while timely graduating them and having their knowledge contributions published—by detailing its manifestations, the strategies adopted to cope with it, and its consequences for both the doctoral students and the scholarly publishing activity system. This chapter explicates the subject-related primary contradiction in the duality of the doctoral students' roles as novice and expert researchers seeking to publish in international journals. It shows how the contradiction was manifested in the doctoral students' developing but still limited grasp and use of some conceptual tools needed for successful scholarly publishing. It illuminates the doctoral students' employment of various mediating resources to tackle the contradiction, and the consequences of their employment of the mediating resources for themselves and for the scholarly publishing activity system. The findings are discussed with reference to the extant literature before the chapter ends with a summary.

5.1 Challenges in Applying Conceptual Tools for Scholarly Publishing

Figure 5.1 shows the tension in the doctoral students' developing but sill limited grasp and use of some conceptual tools needed for successful scholarly publishing (Tension B3). This tension, as noted above, stemmed from the duality of the subject's roles as novice and expert researchers (Tension A2 in Fig. 5.1) (see Hakala, 2009; Sinclair et al., 2014). As will be illustrated below, the tension was reflected most prominently in the doctoral students' difficulties with language, the norms and conventions of scholarly publishing, and the selection of publishable research topics and appropriate research methodology. In order to deal with these difficulties, the doctoral students resorted to an array of mediating resources, including published journal

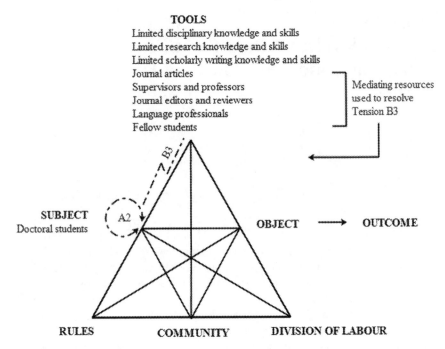

Fig. 5.1 Tools-related tensions concerning scholarly publishing within the doctoral study activity system

articles, textual borrowing and translation, supervisors, fellow students, language professionals, journal editors, and journal reviewers.

As fledgling researchers, the doctoral students had a less-than-desirable grasp and use of a variety of conceptual tools, including language, the rules of the scholarly publishing game, and the selection of publishable research topics and appropriate research methodology, that are crucial for the success of scholarly publishing. Table 5.1 presents a brief summary of the difficulties reported by each of the doctoral students. As can be seen from the table, these difficulties plagued and frequently affected the doctoral students in this study. I further discuss each of them in the following sections.

Limited Language Skills

The most notable difficulty identified by the doctoral students was their limited language skills. All of the doctoral students reported encountering language difficulties publishing in English journals. Professor Liu noted that her students were not well versed in English scholarly writing and some even had difficulties writing intelligibly in English. Liang, for example, admitted that she could not express herself fully and precisely in English. Similarly, Dong found it almost impossible to write directly in English because doing that would distract her from the meanings she was trying to convey and the organisation of the article she had planned. Therefore, she

5.1 Challenges in Applying Conceptual Tools for Scholarly Publishing

Table 5.1 A summary of the doctoral students' difficulties in scholarly publishing[1]

	Limited language skills	Unfamiliarity with the rules of the scholarly publishing game		Inadequate knowledge and skills for conceptualising and designing research	
		Difficulties in selecting appropriate target journals	Difficulties in responding to journal editors and reviewers	Difficulties in choosing publishable research topics	Difficulties in choosing appropriate research methodology
Cui	Yes	Yes	Not reported	Yes	Yes
Dong	Yes	Yes	Yes	Yes	Yes
Fang	Yes	Yes	Yes	Yes	Yes
Liang	Yes	Yes	Not reported	Yes	Not reported
Wei	Yes	Not reported	Yes	Not reported	Yes
Xiao	Yes	Not reported	Yes	Not reported	Yes

first wrote her English manuscript in Chinese and then translated it into English. Cui also reported difficulty in paraphrasing others' words in English scholarly writing:

> If you want to cite others' words, you've got to use your own words. But the problem is that your English writing skills have not reached that level. And there are plagiarism checks. You need to keep clear of ethical problems. (Interview)

Further, Xiao's experience of writing and publishing her first English article exemplified the typical language difficulties encountered by the doctoral students, including both general language problems and specific difficulties with the use of others' words. Xiao wrote an English journal article during her master's study to report on the findings of a study conducted by her supervisor's research team. It took her nearly two years from drafting the article to getting it published, which, according to her, was a process "full of twists and turns" (Xiao, Email). She struggled to compose the initial draft and had to turn to translating, which she also found challenging. As she put it,

> I had no clue about how to translate in the beginning. I first wrote some Chinese sentences about the background of the study. But the problem was I read mostly the English literature. So I had to translate it into Chinese first and then back into English again. After a while, I started to look for the original English sentences and copied them into my draft. Following that, I made some changes to the copied sentences. You know, that was how I came up with the first draft of that article. (Xiao, Interview)

What Xiao described in the latter part of the above excerpt is referred to as patch-writing (Howard, 1992, 1995, 1999) or language reuse (Flowerdew & Li, 2007a, 2007b) in the literature. To deal with the language difficulties, Xiao orchestrated the strategies of translating and borrowing/reusing language from source texts.

---

[1] Reprinted from English for Specific Purposes, 54, Jun Lei and Guangwei Hu, Doctoral candidates' dual role as student and expert scholarly writer: An activity theory perspective, Pages 62–74, Copyright (2019), with permission from Elsevier.

After she finished drafting the article, she submitted it to the *X Journal*, which had one of the highest impact factors among English nursing journals. The outcome of the first round of review from the *X Journal* was "major revision." After two rounds of revision, it was rejected "tragically" (Xiao, Email). She attributed the rejection to her inexperience and slack attitude: "Because that was the first time I submitted a manuscript to an SCI journal, I had no idea about how to respond to reviewers' comments, didn't take it very seriously, and just made some perfunctory revisions" (Xiao, Interview). She then set the manuscript aside for a while as she had to prepare for the oral defence of her master's dissertation. Following her oral defence, she revised it slightly and submitted it to the *Y Journal*. This time it was rejected without even being sent out for review because the topic of her article did not fit the scope of the journal. Then she went on to submit it to the *Z Journal* and the outcome was "even worse" (Xiao, Interview). Her work was checked for plagiarism by the journal and was found to contain many sentences that were lifted verbatim from other journal articles. The editor commented that the manuscript could not be sent out for review unless the copied sentences were rewritten.

These setbacks surely frustrated her. As she put it, "it's impossible to describe how frustrated I was" (Xiao, Email). Overwhelmed by the experience, she went on a summer vacation, "a healing journey," as she put it (Xiao, Interview). Then she was enrolled in the Ph.D. programme and thought that she should not give up on the manuscript since she had already written it up. Hence, she rewrote the copied sentences by reorganising sentence structures and replacing some words and expressions with her own, a strategy that, as noted above, she had also resorted to in drafting the manuscript. Three months later, she submitted the revised version to a new target journal, the *W Journal*, and received the decision letter early next year. The editor's decision was "major revision" because while one reviewer was very interested in her study, the other one suggested that she submit it to another journal. She made the required revisions and resubmitted it, and received the outcome of the second-round of review two months later. One reviewer recommended "accept as is," but a new reviewer provided some suggestions. She made some minor revisions based on the reviewer's suggestions and the manuscript was finally accepted by the journal in the same month.

This experience led her to conclude that "it's REALLY REALLY difficult for a Chinese student to publish an article in an SCI journal" (Xiao, Email). When prompted to reflect on the experience, she highlighted her language difficulties in publishing the article, adding that "it's really difficult to overcome the language hurdles" (Xiao, Interview via QQ). When asked about her views on the journal editors' and reviewers' comments on her language problems, she observed that "all my manuscripts have language problems, so I've got used to reviewers' comments on my language problems" (Xiao, Text-based interview).

Journal editors' and reviewers' comments on the language of the doctoral students' manuscripts provided further evidence of their language difficulties. As confessed by Xiao, all of her English manuscripts had language problems. The following excerpts were some typical comments on the language of her manuscripts:

5.1 Challenges in Applying Conceptual Tools for Scholarly Publishing

> I would also strongly recommend that after the revisions the author(s) contact a licenced translator and request a full review/editing of the English grammar and language. (Editor; Xiao-E MS1-Revision 1)
>
> The content of the manuscript has clearly improved upon revision, but both the original and the newly added text clearly need to be revised by a native English speaker or a professional language editing service. (Editor; Xiao-E MS2-Revision 2)
>
> This manuscript needs a thorough English editorial review. There are many run on sentences and missing prepositions and conjunctions. … This detracts from the valuable information the author is trying to convey. (Reviewer #1; Xiao-E MS3-Revision 1)
>
> There needs to be some tidying up of language in last three paragraphs of this section. (Reviewer #1; Xiao-E MS4-Revision 1)

Likewise, other doctoral students also received similar comments on the language of their manuscripts, as shown in the following excerpts.

> The language is somewhat awkward. Please edit the text. (Editor; Cui-E MS1- Revision 3)
>
> Some international authors whose native language is not English find it helpful to work with a language editing service in the preparation of their papers; some info is available at: ... (Editor; Dong-E MS1-Enquiry about submission)
>
> The whole manuscript needs to be revised to meet the requirements of good English language and style, and finally proofread to correct the wrong use of terms and correct spelling mistakes. (Reviewer #2; Fang-E MS1-Revision 1)
>
> There are many typos, expression and grammatical mistakes. There is a need for major editing in English. (Reviewer #1; Wei-E MS1-Revision 2)

These comments along with the doctoral students' accounts cited above indicated that language problems permeated the doctoral students' English manuscripts and that journal editors and reviewers tended to point out the non-nativeness of the doctoral students and their manuscripts. However, the doctoral students believed that international journal editors and reviewers would rarely reject a submission solely based on language issues. Xiao, for example, remarked that "foreigners [international journal editors and reviewers] seldom reject a manuscript merely because of its language problems" (Text-based interview).

Unfamiliarity with the Rules of the Scholarly Publishing Game

Another salient difficulty faced by the doctoral students related to their unfamiliarity with some of the norms and conventions of scholarly publishing, such as choosing suitable journals and negotiating effectively with journal editors and reviewers. Fang disclosed that in the beginning, she was "a completely blank slate" (Interview) with no clue about major English journals in her field, submission procedures, online submission systems, instructions for authors, or copyright release forms, among many other processes and issues involved in English scholarly publishing. Similarly, Cui's lack of knowledge about proofreading and undue anxiety revealed her unfamiliarity with the norms and expectations of scholarly publishing. She did not know what to do when she was invited to proofread her first English manuscript after it was accepted for publication. She waited anxiously for it to be published after submitting the proofs, worrying that the journal might revoke the acceptance of her manuscript. As she put it, "I'm worried what if they suddenly find my paper poorly written and reject it" (Cui, Interview). Although Cui's undue anxiety might be associated with the high-stakes of the publication and/or her lack of self-confidence, it was also indicative of her unfamiliarity with the norms and conventions of scholarly publishing.

With regard to choosing target journals, Cui observed that without scaffolding from experienced researchers, one may be "completely blind" in choosing the target journal and one could only expect to find the right journal "by sheer accident or luck" (Interview). Professor Liu also noted that some of her students found it difficult to select suitable journals for their manuscripts due to their limited knowledge of the journals in the most relevant and neighbouring fields. As regards negotiating with journal editors and reviewers, Xiao recounted an incident that demonstrated her unfamiliarity with the norms and expectations about responding to journal editors and reviewers. In her responses to the reviewers' comments on her first English article submitted to the *X Journal*, she simply wrote "I disagree with you. I think your comment is wrong [laughs]" (Xiao, Interview). She recalled that one of her fellow students (not included in this study) made the same mistake in her interaction with the editor and reviewers of an English journal—in her responses to the reviewers' comments, she started almost each response with "I disagree." Xiao concluded that "not surprisingly, the manuscript was rejected" (Interview). She ascribed such "laughable" responses to a lack of knowledge and experience in communicating with journal editors and reviewers.

Inadequate Knowledge and Skills for Conceptualising and Designing Research

A third major difficulty encountered by the doctoral students had to do with their limited knowledge and skills for choosing publishable research topics and appropriate research methodologies, such as statistical methods, theoretical frameworks, and data collection and analysis methods. Four of the six doctoral students (i.e., Cui, Dong, Fang, and Liang) underscored the importance and difficulty of choosing publishable research topics for successful scholarly publishing. In Fang's words, "I have come to realise that I must be careful about choosing my research topic if I want to publish it in international journals. I must make sure that my research has some novel elements" (Interview). Cui, in particular, lamented her difficulty in choosing research topics during both her master's and doctoral studies, which she thought severely hindered her progress and productivity. Professor Liu also observed that one of the biggest challenges for doctoral students was to choose publishable research topics.

The doctoral students also reported challenges in choosing appropriate research methodology in their scholarly publishing efforts. Cui admitted that her biggest difficulty in writing English journal articles was conducting statistical analyses. Although she had taken a statistics course, she found that what was prescribed in class or in the textbook could not be applied in practice. Apart from difficulties resulting from the differences between textbook prescriptions and practical applications, the doctoral students also had problems with the different requirements of Chinese and English academic journals. Dong, Fang, and Xiao observed that English journal articles require more information about statistical procedures than Chinese ones. For instance, while English journal articles often report confidence intervals (Fang) and information on the assumptions about some statistical procedures, such as the homogeneity of variance assumption for parametrical tests (Xiao), Chinese ones rarely do. Fang pointed out that "such differences could cause confusion. You wouldn't notice them unless you compare Chinese and English journal articles closely and set out to figure out what they are" (Interview). Furthermore, both Fang and Dong underscored the value of theoretical frameworks in English scholarly publishing and the challenges that Chinese researchers frequently face in applying them in their English scholarly publishing attempts. The main reason for this was linked to their incognizance of Western theories and international publications' favouring of Western theories over those from other parts of the world. Fang, for example, noted that "if you want to get published in English journals, you need to combine your research with international [Western] theoretical frameworks because international journals will not accept parochial theories from China" (Interview).

In addition, the doctoral students also reported difficulties with the methods of data collection and analysis. Fang's example provides a vivid account of such difficulties.

> But I didn't know (much about research methodology) at the time because I read only the Chinese literature. It was all in a mess and all kinds of things were categorised under qualitative research methodology, which seemed high-end, magnificent, and classy (*gao da shang*) yet void and vague. The Chinese literature doesn't delve deeply into specific methodological approaches, nor does it specify which one is appropriate for a particular situation or how data are supposed to be collected and analysed for a certain approach. When I began to write this manuscript [her first English manuscript], I followed the Chinese literature, which was vague. The manuscript was unsurprisingly found flawed by the knowledgeable reviewers. Specifically, I used Method 1 to collect data and Method 2 to analyse the data. According to the standard literature, I should not have used Method 2 to analyse data collected through Method 1. However, the Chinese methodology literature was ambivalent and even conflictual about the differences between the two methods. (Interview)

As a result, when the work was initially submitted to an English journal, it was rejected due to "the fatal methodological flaw" (Fang, Interview).

5.2 Mediating Resources for Coping with the Challenges

As noted above, the doctoral students faced various challenges or tensions in their attempts at scholarly publishing (Tension B3 in Fig. 5.1) because of their limited grasp and use of some conceptual tools needed for successful scholarly publishing. To cope with these challenges, they turned to an array of mediating resources, including journal articles, textual borrowing and translation, journal editors, journal reviewers, supervisors, fellow students, and language professionals. Table 5.2 summarises the doctoral students' reported employment of the various mediating resources to deal with the tensions delineated above. As will be shown below, their deployment of the mediating resources was generally effective in facilitating the attainment of the object of the scholarly publishing activity system: getting published and developing scholarly publishing abilities.

Table 5.2 A summary of the mediating resources for resolving the tensions in scholarly publishing[2]

	Tension (a) Developing and expected language skills and abilities	Tension (b) Developing and expected knowledge of the rules of scholarly publishing	Tension (c) Developing and expected knowledge and skills for conceiving and designing research
Cui	• Editorial services • Journal articles as models • Translation tools	• Did not report	• Supervisor
Dong	• Journal articles as models • Journal editors and reviewers • Language professionals • Translation tools • Writing it in Chinese first and translating it into English later	• Fellow students • Journal editors and reviewers	• Journal editors and reviewers • Statistics textbooks or journal articles • Supervisor
Fang	• Journal articles as models • Language professionals • Translation tools	• Journal editors and reviewers	• Fellow students • Journal editors and reviewers • Statistics textbooks or journal articles • Supervisor
Liang	• Journal articles as models • Translation tools	• Supervisor (Chinese scholarly publishing)	• Did not report
Wei	• Journal articles as models • Language professionals • Supervisor • Translation tools	• Fellow students	• Journal editors and reviewers
Xiao	• Editorial services • Journal articles as models • Language professionals • Supervisor • Translation tools • Writing it in Chinese first and translating it into English later	• Fellow students • Journal editors and reviewers	• Fellow students • Journal editors and reviewers

Coping with Limited Language Skills

The doctoral students adopted several strategies to deal with language difficulties, including using journal articles as model texts, "writing it in Chinese first and translating it into English later", resorting to translation tools, and turning to supervisors, language professionals, or editorial services for help. To begin with, the doctoral

---

[2] Adapted from English for Specific Purposes, 54, Jun Lei and Guangwei Hu, Doctoral candidates' dual role as student and expert scholarly writer: An activity theory perspective, Pages 62–74, Copyright (2019), with permission from Elsevier.

students reported that using journal articles as models or templates was most effective for tackling their language barriers and mastering scholarly writing. Wei, for example, noted that the best way to overcome language difficulties was to read relevant literature extensively and emulate how others write. Likewise, Xiao found it useful to read articles published in high-impact journals to improve her scholarly writing; she collected good sentence structures and useful research methods while reading those articles. She observed that the more she read English journal articles, the more comfortable she became with the English ways of expression.

Dong summarised the strategy succinctly: "Learning to write is essentially imitating. In the beginning, you emulate how journal articles are written and how tables are made in them, or you imitate how your supervisors write by examining their published articles" (Interview). Similarly, Xiao stated that

> I think finding a good model is really important, whether you write in English or in Chinese. For example, after you have decided on your target journal, you have to find an article with similar content to serve as a template for your own writing. I think the most important strategy is to find a template. (Interview)

Another strategy adopted by Dong and Xiao to tackle their language difficulties was writing it in Chinese first and translating it into English later. Dong reported that she had to write her manuscript in Chinese before translating it into English. She felt that writing in English directly would hinder "clear thinking" and/or lead her to wander off the topic. As noted above, Xiao also resorted to this strategy in writing up her first English journal article. However, as her account of that experience indicated, the strategy did not work well and she became increasingly dissatisfied with it because she read mostly in English and had to translate her reading from English into Chinese and then back into English again. Similarly, Dong also grew increasingly dissatisfied with the strategy as she went along.

In response, they dropped the strategy and started to draw upon various conceptual tools and resources and recontextualise them for their own purposes (Li, 2015), as illustrated in the following two excerpts.[3]

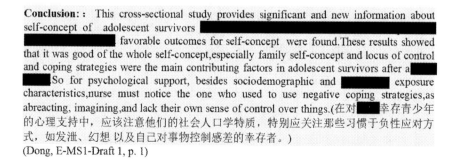

(Dong, E-MS1-Draft 1, p. 1)

---

[3] Reprinted from English for Specific Purposes, 54, Jun Lei, Doctoral candidates' dual role as student and expert scholarly writer: An activity theory perspective, Pages 62–74, Copyright (2019), with permission from Elsevier. Some words and expressions in the excerpts are redacted to ensure anonymity.

Conclusions
This cross-sectional study provides significant and new information about ○○○○ favorable outcomes for self-concept were found in ▇▇▇ 幸存青少年。These results show that ▇ 幸存青少年整体自我概念较好，特别是家庭自我概念，and 心理控制源和应对方式对幸存青少年自我概念的影响较大。
(Dong, E-MS1-Draft 1, p. 12)

As can be seen from the above excerpts, similar to Xiao's earlier account, what Dong did here was not simply "writing it in Chinese first and translating it into English later" but orchestrating the strategies of borrowing or reusing language from English and Chinese source texts (i.e., copying and pasting the Chinese and English source texts) and translating between English and Chinese. While both textual borrowing/language reuse (Flowerdew, 2007; Flowerdew & Li, 2007a; Li, 2006a, 2007) and writing it in one's first language before translating it into English (Duszak & Lewkowicz, 2008; Englander, 2009; Gosden, 1996; Li, 2005; St. John, 1987) have been documented in the literature, the literature has rarely reported an orchestration of these two strategies in the production of the same chunk of text.

Further, although only Dong and Xiao reported using the strategy of "writing it in Chinese first and translating it into English later", all of the doctoral students in this study recounted occasional or frequent use of online translation tools or search engines to deal with their language difficulties. The most popular tools they used included "Google" (https://www.google.com.hk/), "Google Translate" (https://translate.google.com.hk/), "Iciba Online Translation" (http://www.iciba.com/), and "Youdao Translate" (http://fanyi.youdao.com/).[4] Xiao pointed out that the translation tools could provide two types of help with English scholarly writing. First, they could help her check, through sample sentences or texts, grammar rules that she was not sure of. Second, they could help her find words and expressions that she did not know or could not recall. In using translations generated from the translation tools, they all checked and modified them to make sure that grammar and sentence orders were correct. The doctoral students' employment of these strategies indicated that they orchestrated mediating resources and recontextualised them for their own purposes rather than using them separately and mechanically.

A third type of strategy used frequently by the doctoral students to address their language difficulties was seeking assistance from their supervisors (Wei and Xiao), language professionals (Dong, Fang, Wei, and Xiao), and/or editorial services (Cui and Xiao). Wei, for instance, recounted that "after I finish drafting my English manuscript, I often ask my supervisor and my classmates to check whether it has language problems" (Interview). Overall, these mediating resources were successful in assisting the doctoral students in overcoming their language barriers. For example, Dong attributed her success in publishing her first English journal article to an English teacher who helped her revise the article several times. As she put it, "he is my life-saver" (Dong, Text-based interview). In addition, the doctoral students in this study

---

[4] Cui, Dong, Liang, and Xiao found Google and Google Translate to be the best search engine and translation tool. But they had to deal with occasional disruption or blocking of its services in Chinese mainland at the time of this study, which they found frustrating.

valorised English editorial services. Xiao, for instance, regarded English editorial services as essential to the successful publishing of her first English article. She recollected that she had to seek English editorial services because her supervisor for her master's study was "a member of the older generation of academics" (in Xiao's words), was not good at English, and could not help her edit her manuscript. She was then directed to the English editorial services centre by her supervisor. She said that although they made only a small number of changes to her manuscript, the revised version was much better received by the journal editors and reviewers and was finally accepted for publication. The partner university also provided free English editorial services to its doctoral students. Cui spoke highly of the free English editorial services there. These sources of mediating resources and their perceived effectiveness in helping the doctoral students cope with their limited language skills indicate that scholarly publishing is a culturally mediated and socially distributed activity with learning potentials and opportunities for doctoral students.

Useful as these sources of help were, however, they were not without limitations. First, supervisors might not have the time or skill to help their students address their language problems. Xiao, for example, pointed out that despite being very good at English writing skills, her supervisor did not have much time to help her students with their writing because of her heavy administrative responsibilities. Therefore, she usually focused on broad issues rather than language problems, such as the presentation and discussion of findings. In discussing about helping students with their language problems, as delineated in Chap. 4, Professor Liu acknowledged that "supervisors have their own limitations. They also need to seek outside help" (Interview). Specifically, she collaborated with an editorial services provider to tackle her students' language problems. Second, language professionals might be constrained from providing effective language assistance because of their lack of content knowledge. Fang recounted that after she finished drafting her first English manuscript, she asked a native speaker of English to proofread it for her. It turned out that the native English speaker changed only a few prepositions and punctuations. As a result, she underscored the importance of enlisting help from people who are not only good at English but also familiar with disciplinary content. Third, there were some concerns about the accessibility and usefulness of English editorial services despite their apparent usefulness. For one thing, not every supervisor could give their students access to English editing services. Fang observed that unlike some of her fellow students (i.e., Professor Liu's students) who had their own language editorial team to help them polish their manuscripts before submission, she had to do everything by herself. For another, as both Professor Liu and Dong discovered, the quality of English editorial services varied widely, and it was difficult to find quality and trustworthy English editorial services providers. Furthermore, Dong and Fang pointed out that doctoral students might find it a big burden to pay for editorial fees if the services are not free and their supervisor or the university does not reimburse the fees.

Addressing Unfamiliarity with the Rules of the Scholarly Publishing Game

The doctoral students relied primarily on their supervisor, fellow students, and journal editors to cope with their unfamiliarity with the norms and conventions of scholarly publishing, especially in selecting appropriate target journals and responding appropriately to journal editors and reviewers. Liang's experience of publishing one of her Chinese articles exemplified the role that supervisors could play in helping their students choose the most suitable journals for their manuscripts. After her first submission to a journal was rejected, she consulted her supervisor about what to do next. Her supervisor suggested that she submit it to another journal, explaining that the editor of the latter journal had different visions and tastes from the previous one and would most likely find the strengths in her article. Following her supervisor's suggestion, she submitted it to the journal without any revisions. As expected by her supervisor, the editor accepted it for publication after only some minor revisions.

Fellow students constituted another important source of information on the norms and expectations of scholarly publishing. Dong observed that her fellow students and friends who had published English journal articles helped her the most with her English scholarly writing. She asked them for information and suggestions about potential target journals for her manuscript, what the reviewing process was like, and how to respond to journal editors' and reviewers' comments. She found such information "invaluable" in that it helped her learn about the procedures, requirements, and expectations of scholarly publishing, and successfully navigate through the publishing process. Aside from such informal sharing, supervisors also organised seminars for published students to share their experiences with their fellow students. Xiao, for example, recalled that after one of her seniors published an article in an SCI journal, her master's supervisor organised a seminar for her to share her experience of publishing that article, covering such topics as the processes of submitting to different journals, revising the manuscript, and responding to reviewers' comments. Her master's supervisor asked everyone else present to share their thoughts and ideas before she made some final comments. Xiao spoke highly of such sharing among fellow students in enhancing her knowledge of the norms and expectations of scholarly publishing. There were also such seminars in the Nursing Department, though, as discussed in Chap. 4, they were not held as regularly and systematically as the doctoral students would like them to be.

Furthermore, journal editors and reviewers also played a vital role in inducting students into the norms and expectations governing scholarly publishing. Both Fang and Xiao turned to journal editors to familiarise themselves with the norms and expectations of scholarly publishing. As noted above, Xiao made a "laughable" (to her) mistake of bluntly rejecting the reviewer's comments on her first English manuscript. Luckily, in the decision letter, the editor urged her to respect the reviewer even if she disagreed with him or her. Ever since then, Xiao has been extremely careful in responding to journal editors' and reviewers' comments. Her strategy was to thank the reviewers or editors whether she agreed or disagreed with them. For example, she prefaced with a "thank you" in almost all her responses to the editors' and reviewers' comments on her second English manuscript. The following excerpts are some of her typical responses.

5.2 Mediating Resources for Coping with the Challenges

Reviewer #1's general comments:

The article addresses an important question, research methods are adequate but the article needs copy editing for language and ensuring systematic referencing.

Response:

Thanks for pointing out the grammatical problems in this paper, and it is really difficult for us to write an English paper as Chinese. We appreciate with the wonderful recommendations and have invited a professional translator to browse and revise the grammatical issues. We hope the language issues have improved and we will continue to ameliorate them. We expect that you could give us more suggestions about grammar and language issues.

Reviewer #2's detailed comments:

1. Page 4 line 17 - 19: this second section of data from the ... does not add much to the data immediately preceding it.

Response:

We strongly appreciate the suggestion and delete the reference (page 4, line 17).

As these excerpts indicate, Xiao obviously took the editor's suggestion to heart and developed a strategic (and perhaps too accommodationist) sense of the negotiation processes involved in scholarly publishing. In addition, she also asked the editors or reviewers for more suggestions in some cases. For instance, in her response to Reviewer 1's General Comments quoted above, she wrote that "we expect that you could give us more suggestions about grammar and language issues." When asked in a follow-up interview about her rationale for similar expressions in her revisions of another manuscript (E MS3), she said:

> That was based on my experience publishing my first SCI article. The reviewers may make many suggestions and some of them may be very difficult to address, and you have no idea whether they would find your responses satisfactory. So if you ask them for more suggestions, they may give you another chance even if they find your responses unsatisfactory. Personally, I find this strategy very effective. The reviewers will feel 'gaining face' (flattered) because you respect them. (Xiao, Text-based interview)

Fang also thought highly of the role played by the editor of an international journal in helping her learn about the rules of publishing in English journals. The editor was invited to talk about how to get published in SCI journals at a conference held at the focal university, when Fang was just enrolled in the Ph.D. programme. The editor's talk covered not only the procedures and strategies for scholarly publishing but also the important role of resilience in scholarly publishing. She exhorted the audience to neither overestimate nor underestimate their chances of getting published, and to persevere in their scholarly publishing eandeavours. Each of Fang's two English manuscripts was rejected seven or eight times. Each rejection was understandably frustrating. Therefore, Fang would not have succeeded without resilience, and she saw it playing a critical role in her success at publishing her two English manuscripts.

The above accounts show that the doctoral students drew on informal help from their supervisors, fellow students, and journal editors and reviewers to deal with their unfamiliarity with the rules of the publishing game. This again points to the socially distributed nature of scholarly publishing and the learning opportunities that it could afford to doctoral students.

Tackling Inadequate Knowledge and Skills for Conceptualising and Designing Research

To tackle their inadequate knowledge and skills for conceptualising and designing research—i.e., choosing publishable research topics and appropriate research methodologies, the doctoral students turned to supervisors (Cui, Dong, and Fang), statistics textbooks and journal articles (Dong and Fang), and/or journal editors and reviewers (Dong, Fang, Wei, and Xiao). Dong observed that supervisors could help students ensure that their research topics are "cutting-edge, scientific, and feasible" (Interview). In contrast to her difficulty finding publishable research topics on her own, Cui envied one of her classmates, because her supervisor (Professor Liu) gave research topics to her and provided her with specific directions for writing. She characterised the collaboration as "harmonious and effective" (Cui, Interview). As pointed out in Chap. 3, supervisors' knowledge about the nature of the nursing discipline, the hot topics in the field, and the rules of the scholarly publishing game could play a pivotal role in choosing publishable research topics. Specifically, Professor Liu assigned her students to work on the health and care of trauma survivors for their publications. The health and care of trauma survivors, according to Professor Liu, was a new and cutting-edge topic. On the one hand, research on this topic tended to have good chances of being accepted by international journals. On the other hand, the Nursing Department had some unique advantages to conduct research on the topic because its expertise and unique geographical location.

In addition, Fang reported that she asked her supervisor to check her manuscript for its methodology, the trustworthiness of its conclusion, and the insightfulness of its discussion. Dong recounted her experience of consulting statistics textbooks and journal articles for advice and information on statistical methods.

> You've got to keep trying. Sometimes, you need to read statistics textbooks and journal articles using the same and similar methods. Of course, that would take you more time.... But it is just a matter of 'drawing a painting of a gourd ladle with a gourd as a model' (*zhao hulu hua piao*, imitating or copying). (Interview)

Further, the doctoral students also resorted to journal editors and reviewers for methodological assistance. For instance, in addressing problems with data collection and analysis in her first English article, Fang was lucky to receive comments from a journal reviewer on her second English manuscript, which used the same qualitative approach as her first English manuscript. The reviewer recommended several references on research methodology to her. She downloaded all the recommended references and googled the author of the references, finding that she was an expert on the methodological approach. Therefore, she downloaded all of her articles and read them closely. By doing so, she not only successfully addressed the methodological problems in the two manuscripts, but also obtained a good knowledge of the research approach and related methods.

5.3 Constraints and Affordances of Doctoral Publication

This chapter has examined the primary contradiction within the subject component concerning the dual roles of the doctoral students as student researchers and as expert researchers in scholarly publishing during candidature. This duality of doctoral students' roles is well captured by the notion of "researcher PhD students," who "are expected to act as independent and productive researchers even before attaining the Ph.D. degree" (Hakala, 2009, p. 501). As Hakala and many others (Aitchison & Lee, 2006; Caffarella & Barnett, 2000; Can & Walker, 2011; Mizzi, 2014; Sinclair et al., 2014) have pointed out, these dual roles for doctoral students are apparently contradictory. In the present study, this contradiction was manifested most saliently in the doctoral students' limited grasp and use of some conceptual tools needed for successful scholarly publishing, including limited language skills, unfamiliarity with the rules of the publishing game, and inadequate knowledge and skills for conceptualising and designing research.

As for their limited language skills, all of the six doctoral students recounted having language difficulties in their English scholarly publishing endeavours. Their language difficulties included not only such surface problems as diction and grammar but also more complex ones, such as expressing ideas precisely and concisely and paraphrasing source texts. In addition, they also received journal editors' and reviewers' comments on their language problems that drew attention to the non-nativeness of themselves and their manuscripts. Notwithstanding their awareness of their language problems and journal editors' and reviewers' comments on them, they did not believe that their manuscripts would be rejected solely based on language problems. These findings are largely consistent with those from previous studies (e.g., Cho, 2009; Englander, 2009; Ferguson et al., 2011; Flowerdew, 1999a, 1999b, 2001; Gosden, 1992; Mišak et al., 2005; see Uzuner, 2008, for a review of studies on this), which have found that EAL researchers tend to encounter language problems in their scholarly publishing efforts, especially in more complex textual practices. Comments by journal editors and reviewers on the non-nativeness of the doctoral students and their manuscripts resemble those on EAL researchers and their submissions to international journals documented in the literature (e.g., Belcher, 2007; Flowerdew, 2000, 2001; Lillis & Curry, 2010). Those comments also pointed out the non-nativeness of EAL researchers and their manuscripts, and recommended that EAL researchers seek help from native speakers of English. The doctoral students' perceptions regarding how their language might affect the acceptance or rejection of their manuscripts are consonant with the findings of some studies (Gosden, 2003; Mišak et al., 2005), but dissonant with those from others (Cho, 2009; Duszak & Lewkowicz, 2008; Kaplan, 2001; Kubota, 2003).

In addition to language challenges, the doctoral students reported unfamiliarity with some of the rules of the scholarly publishing game, especially choosing appropriate journals for their manuscripts and responding appropriately and effectively to journal editors and reviewers. This finding concurs with those from the previous research (e.g., Berkenkotter & Huckin, 1995; Cho, 2004; Gosden, 1996; Li, 2006a), which have revealed that novice researchers are generally unaware about some basic but important norms and conventions of scholarly publishing. One possible reason why doctoral students tend to find it particularly difficult to grapple with some of the norms and conventions might be that these norms and conventions are tacit and thus not readily amenable to articulation (e.g., Bazerman, 2009; Blakeslee, 1997; Flowerdew, 2015; Kwan, 2010, 2013; Paré et al., 2011; Starke-Meyerring, 2011). Furthermore, the doctoral students also highlighted their inadequate knowledge and skills for choosing publishable research topics and appropriate research methodologies. In this regard, previous research has noted that both topic selection (Duszak & Lewkowicz, 2008; Hasrati & Street, 2009; Lei & Hu, 2015) and methodological issues (Gosden, 2003; Mišak et al., 2005)—including the privileging of Centre theories in international journals (Canagarajah, 2002a; Duszak & Lewkowicz, 2008; Flowerdew, 2001; Lillis & Curry, 2010)—are common reasons for the rejection of manuscripts.

The findings discussed above indicate that the doctoral students encountered similar difficulties and constraints to those faced by EAL researchers. They also lend support to Kwan's (2010, 2013) framework for scholarly publishing competence that includes the ability to conceptualise and design research as a crucial component (see also Altbach, 2009; Belcher, 2007; Hasrati & Street, 2009; Lei & Hu, 2015). Therefore, together with the findings from Chap. 4 that have highlighted the importance of output planning and managing and interweaving publication with other activity systems in successful scholarly publishing during doctoral candidature, the findings of this study confirm Kwan's (2010, 2013; see also Watson, 2012) framework for scholarly publishing repertoire, which consists of writing manuscripts, handling reviews, planning and managing research output, aligning publication and thesis, and conceptualising and designing publishable research. This suggests that from some doctoral students' and supervisors' perspectives, scholarly publishing involves not only writing but other repertoires of knowledge and skills as well.

To tackle the above challenges, the doctoral students resorted to various mediating resources, including journal articles, textual borrowing and translation, journal editors, journal reviewers, fellow students, supervisors, and language professionals. These findings generally corroborate the findings from previous research (see, e.g., Burrough-Boenisch, 2003; Gosden, 1996; Li & Flowerdew, 2007) that has examined EAL researchers' strategies to cope with language difficulties. This suggests that doctoral publication is replete with not only constraints but also affordances.

Taking the strategies for coping with the language problems as a case in point, frequent use of journal articles as models by EAL researchers has been documented in several studies (e.g., Buckingham, 2008; Casanave & Vandrick, 2003; Li, 2005, 2007). Similarly, the strategy of writing a manuscript in one's first language before translating it into English has also been reported in the literature (e.g., Duszak & Lewkowicz, 2008; Englander, 2009; Gosden, 1996; Li, 2005; St. John, 1987), and the EAL researchers in previous studies were also found to become increasingly dissatisfied with the strategy and finally drop it (see Gosden, 1996; Li, 2005; St. John, 1987).

In addition, the findings regarding the roles of supervisors, language professors, and editorial services in helping doctoral students cope with their language problems are also largely consistent with those from the previous research (see, e.g., Burrough-Boenisch, 2003; Li & Flowerdew, 2007), which found that these sources of mediating resources provide generally effective language assistance, though they each have their limitations, too. Specifically, several previous studies reported supervisors' inclination to focus on the content rather than language of manuscripts (Burrough-Boenisch, 2003; Lillis & Curry, 2006a) and their limited ability to help their students with language problems (Bazerman, 2009; Kwan, 2010, 2013; Lei & Hu, 2015; Li & Cargill, 2019; Paré, 2010).

Similarly, previous research has also revealed language professionals' limitations in providing language support because of their lack of content knowledge (Burrough-Boenisch, 2003; Cho, 2004; Li & Flowerdew, 2007; Mišak et al., 2005) and the surprising scarcity and the staggering cost of quality and reliable English editorial services in Chinese mainland (see Li & Flowerdew, 2007). As shown in this study, although the number of English editorial services providers seemed to have increased substantially since Li and Flowerdew's (2007) observation, the high cost and low quality of such services appear to remain unchanged.

However, the strategy of reusing and translating both Chinese and English source texts and recontextualising them for one's own purposes, employed by Dong and Xiao in this study, has been rarely reported in the literature. A possible reason for this might be the relatively scant research attention to manuscript drafting in previous research on scholarly publishing. Therefore, the drafting strategy identified in this study in particular and strategies for manuscript drafting in general are both worthy of further research.

These findings indicate that scholarly publishing is a socially distributed and culturally mediated activity (Lundell & Beach, 2003; Prior & Shipka, 2003; Simpson, 2013) and that it carries along affordances for doctoral students not only to learn the ropes of scholarly publishing but also to become increasingly fuller members of the target discourse communities (Mizzi, 2014; Paré, 2010). Notably, the cultural artefacts and social others involved in doctoral students' scholarly publishing activities embody the traditions, norms, and conventions of scholarly publishing in the discipline (Kamler, 2008; Paré, 2010; Starke-Meyerring, 2011). Therefore, through interacting with them, doctoral students can be socialised into not only the game of scholarly publishing but also the academic culture and community (Mizzi, 2014; Paré, 2010). As Mizzi (2014, p. 55) points out, because of the assistance from journal editors, reviewers, supervisors, and others, doctoral students' scholarly publishing processes are well-supplied with "pedagogical opportunities." This finding seems to contradict the findings reported in Chap. 4 that the strategies adopted by the doctoral students to cope with their time constraints took a product-oriented approach to scholarly publishing and truncated their opportunities to learn the ropes of scholarly publishing. This contradiction is a manifestation of the dialectical relationship between the product-oriented and the process-oriented approaches to the object of the scholarly publishing activity system. Thus, the process-oriented approach and the product-oriented approach are not to be interpreted as dichotomous (see Chap. 6

for a more detailed discussion about this). The same holds true for doctoral students' dual roles as student and expert researchers in their scholarly publishing efforts.

5.4 Conclusion

This chapter has explicated the subject-related contradiction concerning the doctoral students' dual roles as student researchers and as expert researchers in terms of scholarly publishing during doctoral candidature. The findings have shown that this subject-related primary contradiction was manifested most prominently in the doctoral students' developing but still limited grasp and use of some conceptual tools needed for successful scholarly publishing. The challenges arising from the doctoral students' limited grasp and use of the conceptual tools have revealed successful scholarly publishing as requiring a multi-faceted repertoire of knowledge, skills, and strategies for writing manuscripts, handling reviews, conceptualising and designing publishable research, planning and managing research output, and interweaving publication with other activities. The strategies that the doctoral students employed to deal with those challenges underscore doctoral students' dual and evolving roles as student and expert researchers. They suggest that scholarly publishing is a culturally-mediated and socially-mediated activity not only fraught with constraints but also rich in affordances for learning and identity development.

References

Aitchison, C., & Lee, A. (2006). Research writing: Problems and pedagogies. *Teaching in Higher Education, 11*, 265–278. https://doi.org/10.1080/13562510600680574
Altbach, P. G. (2009). Peripheries and centers: Research universities in developing countries. *Asia Pacific Education Review, 10*, 15–27. https://doi.org/10.1007/s12564-009-9000-9
Bazerman, C. (2009). Genre and cognitive development: Beyond writing to learn. In C. Bazerman, A. Bonin, & D. Figueiredo (Eds.), *Genre in a changing world* (pp. 279–294). The WAC Clearinghouse.
Belcher, D. (2007). Seeking acceptance in an English-only research world. *Journal of Second Language Writing, 16*, 1–22. https://doi.org/10.1016/j.jslw.2006.12.001
Berkenkotter, C., & Huckin, T. N. (1995). *Genre knowledge in disciplinary communication: Cognition/culture/power*. Lawrence Erlbaum.
Blakeslee, A. M. (1997). Activity, context, interaction, and authority. *Journal of Business and Technical Communication, 11*, 125–169. https://doi.org/10.1177/1050651997011002001
Buckingham, L. (2008). Development of English academic writing competence by Turkish scholars. *International Journal of Doctoral Studies, 3*, 1–18.
Burrough-Boenisch, J. (2003). Shapers of published NNS research articles. *Journal of Second Language Writing, 12*, 223–243. https://doi.org/10.1016/s1060-3743(03)00037-7
Caffarella, R. S., & Barnett, B. G. (2000). Teaching doctoral students to become scholarly writers: The importance of giving and receiving critiques. *Studies in Higher Education, 25*, 39–52. https://doi.org/10.1080/030750700116000

References

Can, G., & Walker, A. (2011). A model for doctoral students' perceptions and attitudes toward written feedback for academic writing. *Research in Higher Education, 52*, 508–536. https://doi.org/10.1007/s11162-010-9204-1

Canagarajah, A. S. (2002a). *A geopolitics of academic writing.* University of Pittsburgh Press.

Casanave, C. P., & Vandrick, S. (2003). Introduction: Issues in writing for publication. In C. P. Casanave & S. Vandrick (Eds.), *Writing for scholarly publication: Behind the scenes in language education* (pp. 1–16). Lawrence Erlbaum.

Cho, D. W. (2009). Science journal paper writing in an EFL context: The case of Korea. *English for Specific Purposes, 28*, 230–239. https://doi.org/10.1016/j.esp.2009.06.002

Cho, S. (2004). Challenges of entering discourse communities through publishing in English: Perspectives of nonnative-speaking doctoral students in the United States of America. *Journal of Language, Identity & Education, 3*, 47–72. https://doi.org/10.1207/s15327701jlie0301_3

Duszak, A., & Lewkowicz, J. (2008). Publishing academic texts in English: A Polish perspective. *Journal of English for Academic Purposes, 7*, 108–120. https://doi.org/10.1016/j.jeap.2008.03.001

Englander, K. (2009). Transformation of the identities of nonnative English-speaking scientists as a consequence of the social construction of revision. *Journal of Language, Identity & Education, 8*, 35–53. https://doi.org/10.1080/15348450802619979

Ferguson, G., Pérez-Llantada, C., & Plo, R. (2011). English as an international language of scientific publication: A study of attitudes. *World Englishes, 30*, 41–59. https://doi.org/10.1111/j.1467-971X.2010.01656.x

Flowerdew, J., & Li, Y. (2007b). Plagiarism and second language writing in an electronic age. *Annual Review of Applied Linguistics, 27*, 161–183. https://doi.org/10.1017/S0267190508070086

Flowerdew, J. (1999a). Problems in writing for scholarly publication in English: The case of Hong Kong. *Journal of Second Language Writing, 8*, 243–264. https://doi.org/10.1016/s1060-3743(99)80116-7

Flowerdew, J. (1999b). Writing for scholarly publication in English: The case of Hong Kong. *Journal of Second Language Writing, 8*, 123–145. https://doi.org/10.1016/s1060-3743(99)80125-8

Flowerdew, J. (2000). Discourse community, legitimate peripheral participation, and the nonnative-English-speaking scholar. *TESOL Quarterly, 34*, 127–150. https://doi.org/10.2307/3588099

Flowerdew, J. (2001). Attitudes of journal editors to nonnative speaker contributions. *TESOL Quarterly, 35*, 121–150. https://doi.org/10.2307/3587862

Flowerdew, J. (2007). The non-Anglophone scholar on the periphery of scholarly publication. *AILA Review, 20*, 14–27. https://doi.org/10.1075/aila.20.04flo

Flowerdew, J. (2015). Some thoughts on English for Research Publication Purposes (ERPP) and related issues. *Language Teaching, 48*, 250–262. https://doi.org/10.1017/S0261444812000523

Flowerdew, J., & Li, Y. (2007a). Language re-use among Chinese apprentice scientists writing for publication. *Applied Linguistics, 28*, 440–465. https://doi.org/10.1093/applin/amm031

Gosden, H. (1992). Research writing and NNSs: From the editors. *Journal of Second Language Writing, 1*, 123–139. https://doi.org/10.1016/1060-3743(92)90012-e

Gosden, H. (1996). Verbal reports of Japanese novices' research writing practices in English. *Journal of Second Language Writing, 5*, 109–128. https://doi.org/10.1016/s1060-3743(96)90021-1

Gosden, H. (2003). 'Why not give us the full story?': Functions of referees' comments in peer reviews of scientific research papers. *Journal of English for Academic Purposes, 2*, 87–101. https://doi.org/10.1016/s1475-1585(02)00037-1

Hakala, J. (2009). Socialization of junior researchers in new academic research environments: Two case studies from Finland. *Studies in Higher Education, 34*, 501–516. https://doi.org/10.1080/03075070802597119

Hasrati, M., & Street, B. (2009). PhD topic arrangement in 'D'iscourse communities of engineers and social sciences/humanities. *Journal of English for Academic Purposes, 8*, 14–25. https://doi.org/10.1016/j.jeap.2009.01.002

Howard, R. M. (1992). A plagiarism pentimento. *Journal of Teaching Writing, 11*, 233–245.

Howard, R. M. (1995). Plagiarisms, authorships, and the academic death penalty. *College English, 57,* 788–806. https://doi.org/10.2307/378403

Howard, R. M. (1999). *Standing in the shadow of giants: Plagiarists, authors, collaborators.* Ablex.

Kamler, B. (2008). Rethinking doctoral publication practices: Writing from and beyond the thesis. *Studies in Higher Education, 33,* 283–294. https://doi.org/10.1080/03075070802049236

Kaplan, R. B. (2001). English—the accidental language of science? In U. Ammon (Ed.), *The dominance of English as a language of science: Effects on other languages and language communities* (pp. 3–26). Mouton de Gruyter.

Kubota, R. (2003). Striving for original voice in publication?: A critical reflection. In C. P. Casanave & S. Vandrick (Eds.), *Writing for scholarly publication: Behind the scenes in language education* (pp. 73–83). Lawrence Erlbaum.

Kwan, B. S. C. (2010). An investigation of instruction in research publishing offered in doctoral programs: The Hong Kong case. *Higher Education, 59,* 55–68. https://doi.org/10.1007/s10734-009-9233-x

Kwan, B. S. C. (2013). Facilitating novice researchers in project publishing during the doctoral years and beyond: A Hong Kong-based study. *Studies in Higher Education, 38,* 207–225. https://doi.org/10.1080/03075079.2011.576755

Lei, J., & Hu, G. (2015). Apprenticeship in scholarly publishing: A student perspective on doctoral supervisors' roles. *Publications, 3,* 27–42. https://doi.org/10.3390/publications3010027

Li, Y. (2005). Multidimensional enculturation: The case of an EFL Chinese doctoral student. *Journal of Asian Pacific Communication, 15,* 153–170. https://doi.org/10.1075/japc.15.1.10li

Li, Y. (2006). A doctoral student of physics writing for publication: A sociopolitically-oriented case study. *English for Specific Purposes, 25,* 456–478. https://doi.org/10.1016/j.esp.2005.12.002

Li, Y. (2007). Apprentice scholarly writing in a community of practice: An intraview of an NNES graduate student writing a research article. *TESOL Quarterly, 41,* 55–79. https://doi.org/10.1002/j.1545-7249.2007.tb00040.x

Li, Y. (2015). 'Standing on the shoulders of giants': Recontextualization in writing from sources. *Science and Engineering Ethics, 21,* 1–18. https://doi.org/10.1007/s11948-014-9590-4

Li, Y., & Cargill, M. (2019). Seeking supervisor collaboration in a school of sciences at a Chinese university. In K. Hyland & L. Wong (Eds.), *Specialised English: New directions in ESP and EAP research and practice* (pp. 240–252). Routledge.

Li, Y., & Flowerdew, J. (2007). Shaping Chinese novice scientists' manuscripts for publication. *Journal of Second Language Writing, 16,* 100–117. https://doi.org/10.1016/j.jslw.2007.05.001

Lillis, T., & Curry, M. J. (2010). *Academic writing in a global context: The politics and practices of publishing in English.* Routledge.

Lillis, T., & Curry, M. J. (2006). Professional academic writing by multilingual scholars: Interactions with literacy brokers in the production of English-medium texts. *Written Communication, 23,* 3–35. https://doi.org/10.1177/0741088305283754

Lundell, D. B., & Beach, R. (2003). Dissertation writers' negotiations with competing activity systems. In C. Bazerman & D. Russell (Eds.), *Writing selves/writing societies* (pp. 483–514). The WAC Clearinghouse.

Mišak, A., Marušić, M., & Marušić, A. (2005). Manuscript editing as a way of teaching academic writing: Experience from a small scientific journal. *Journal of Second Language Writing, 14,* 122–131. https://doi.org/10.1016/j.jslw.2005.05.001

Mizzi, R. C. (2014). Writing realities: An exploration of drawbacks and benefits of publishing while enrolled in a doctoral program. *New Horizons in Adult Education and Human Resource Development, 26,* 54–59. https://doi.org/10.1002/nha3.20063

Paré, A. (2010). Slow the presses: Concerns for premature publication. In C. Aitchison, B. Kamler, & A. Lee (Eds.), *Publishing pedagogies for the doctorate and beyond* (pp. 30–46). Routledge.

Paré, A., Starke-Meyerring, D., & McAlpine, L. (2011). Knowledge and identity work in the supervision of doctoral student writing: Shaping rhetorical subjects. In D. Starke-Meyerring, A. Paré, N. Artemeva, M. Horne, & L. Yousoubova (Eds.), *Writing in knowledge societies* (pp. 215–236). Parlor Press and WAC Clearinghouse.

References

Prior, P., & Shipka, J. (2003). Chronotropic lamination: Tracing the contours of literate activity. In C. Bazerman & D. R. Russell (Eds.), *Writing selves/Writing societies: Research from activity perspectives* (pp. 180–238). The WAC Clearinghous.

Simpson, S. (2013). Systems of writing response: A Brazilian student's experiences writing for publication in an environmental sciences doctoral program. *Research in the Teaching of English, 48,* 228–249.

Sinclair, J., Barnacle, R., & Cuthbert, D. (2014). How the doctorate contributes to the formation of active researchers: What the research tells us. *Studies in Higher Education, 39,* 1972–1986. https://doi.org/10.1080/03075079.2013.806460

St. John, M. J. (1987). Writing processes of Spanish scientists publishing in English. *English for Specific Purposes, 6,* 113–120. https://doi.org/10.1016/0889-4906(87)90016-0

Starke-Meyerring, D. (2011). The paradox of writing in doctoral education: Student experiences. In L. McAlpine & C. Amundsen (Eds.), *Doctoral education: Research-based strategies for doctoral students, supervisors and administrators* (pp. 75–95). Springer.

Uzuner, S. (2008). Multilingual scholars' participation in core/global academic communities: A literature review. *Journal of English for Academic Purposes, 7,* 250–263. https://doi.org/10.1016/j.jeap.2008.10.007

Watson, M. (Ed.). (2012). *Publication practices and multilingual professionals in US universities: Towards critical perspectives on administration and pedagogy.* The WAC Clearinghouse.

Chapter 6
Conclusion

The book has drawn on sociopolitical perspectives to explore policies, practices, and identities pertaining to a group of Chinese nursing doctoral students' scholarly publishing experiences and practices. In the preceding three chapters, I have reported on the findings of this study. In Chap. 3, I delineated the institutional policies and the major stakeholders' perspectives on doctoral publication, and provided an overview of the object-related and the subject-related primary contradictions that the doctoral students encountered in their scholarly publishing activities. Then in Chaps. 4 and 5, I examined the object-related and the subject-related contradictions, respectively, elucidating their manifestations, the strategies adopted to cope with them, and the impacts of the adopted strategies on the doctoral students and the scholarly publishing activity system. In this chapter, I summarise the major findings of the study and highlight its contributions, focusing on connections between policies, practices, and identities, and putting forward a situated conceptualisation of doctoral publication based on the findings of this study. Then I outline the limitations of this study and identify several directions for future research before I conclude the book by discussing the implications of this study for theory, policy, and pedagogy.

6.1 Connections Between Policies, Practices, and Identities

This study has revealed that the doctoral students were engaged in a network of activities (Engeström, 1987, 2000; Engeström et al., 1995; Kuutti, 1996; Leont'ev, 1978/2009; Roth & Lee, 2007). Specifically, their scholarly publishing activity systems nested and interacted with activity systems not only within (e.g., the coursework activity system, the thesis research activity system) but also beyond (e.g., the master's study activity system, the professional work activity system) the overarching doctoral study activity system (Beauchamp et al., 2009; Lundell & Beach, 2003; Russell, 1997). For instance, Xiao's scholarly publishing activity system started from her master's study at another university and was carried over into her doctoral study at the focal university. Likewise, Fang's scholarly publishing activity system originated from her professional work and started long before her enrolment in the doctoral programme. A conclusion that can be drawn from these findings is that the activity settings for doctoral students' scholarly publishing activities are complicated and dynamic and that the activity system of scholarly publishing during doctoral candidature is, as unfolded in this study, chronotopically laminated or dispersed across "places, times, people, and artifacts" (Prior & Shipka, 2003, p. 181; see also Prior, 1994, 1997, 1998; Prior & Min, 2008).

As regards policies on doctoral publication, this study has shown that the university's publication requirements and incentive schemes are characteristic of neoliberal ideologies and impinge on doctoral students' publishing practices and evolving identities. The study has found that apart from meeting the university's publication requirements, the major stakeholders (i.e., the university, supervisor, doctoral student) had an array of heterogeneous motives, including ensuring the quality of the doctoral programme and degree, improving doctoral students' scholarly abilities, preparing them for their future careers, and contributing to knowledge. As noted in Chap. 3, these motives revolved around the two main objectives of doctoral education, namely, the production of knowledge and the reproduction of knowledge producers (Aitchison et al., 2012; Boud & Lee, 2009; Delamont et al., 2000; Kamler, 2008; Kandiko & Kinchin, 2012; McGrail et al., 2006; Parry, 2007).

In addition, these long-term collective objectives notwithstanding, all the major stakeholders placed a premium on the product and outcome of the activity systems of scholarly publishing and doctoral education. The university, for example, adopted a stick-and-carrot approach to motivating the doctoral students to publish during their candidature, with the publication requirements being the stick and the reward schemes being the carrot. This prevailing stress on product and outcome as opposed to process and experience was related to the increased emphasis on performance and efficiency engendered by the ever-accelerating globalisation and marketisation of higher education over the past few decades (Aitchison et al., 2010; Lee & Lee, 2013; Sinclair et al., 2014; Starfield, 2004).

Furthermore, as discussed in Chap. 5, such an overriding focus on product and outcome triggered changes in the object, rules, and division of labour in the scholarly publishing activity system, which in turn restructured the major stakeholders' actions accordingly. As a result, the reshaped actions of the doctoral students, the supervisor, and the university undermined the doctoral students' opportunities to learn scholarly publishing and reinforced the prevalent product-oriented object. For example, in adopting the orchestrating strategy, the division of labour of the scholarly publishing activity was changed with the result that the doctoral students were engaged in only part of the actions of scholarly publishing and that their opportunities to learn the trade of scholarly publishing were undercut. Additionally, the students' motives for getting published and for learning scholarly publishing, as shown in Chap. 5, prompted them to draw on various mediating resources, thereby facilitating their participation in the scholarly publishing activity. On the basis of these findings, it is possible to conclude that the major stakeholders' motives for scholarly publishing have a bearing on and

6.1 Connections Between Policies, Practices, and Identities

can both constrain and enable doctoral students' scholarly publishing practices and evolving identities.

This study has demonstrated that the doctoral students encountered two primary contradictions in their scholarly publishing endeavours, namely, the object-related and the subject-related primary contradictions. The object-related primary contradiction concerned the duality of the object of the scholarly publishing activity system, i.e., developing the doctoral students into autonomous researchers while timely graduating them and having their research published. As shown in Chaps. 4 and 5, the product and outcome aspects of the object were given priority over the process and experience aspects of the object because of the performativity and audit culture prevailing in the focal university, the competing demands on the doctoral students, and the inadequate process-oriented support from the university and the supervisors. The subject-related challenges related to the doctoral students' dual roles as student researchers and as expert researchers, which has been characterised by Simpson (2013) as "writing publishable articles as a graduate student and writing for publication as an established researcher" (p. 243). For this reason, the doctoral students found themselves in a double bind or "suspended between two stools" (Delamont et al., 1994, cited in Collinson, 2006, p. 275) in the sense that they were supposed to learn the trade of scholarly publishing, but at the same time, they were also expected to function as expert researchers who are able to "conduct academic research independently" and "make a novel contribution to science and technology" ("The University Regulations for Doctoral Education").

The study has shown that as primary contradictions, both the object-related and the subject-related contradictions were dialectical and structural. From an activity theory perspective, primary contradictions denote two "nonidentical expressions of the same category" and thus reflect dialectical relationships (Roth & Lee, 2007, p. 195). Therefore, these contradictions do not manifest themselves but are reflected in secondary contradictions (Bonneau, 2013; Engeström, 1987; Foot, 2014). Moreover, because of their dialectical nature, primary contradictions cannot be completely resolved (Cole & Engeström, 1993; Engeström, 1987, 1999, 2001; Engeström & Miettinen, 1999; Roth & Lee, 2007). Furthermore, contradictions in activity theory can both impede and facilitate learning and development. The findings of this study have evinced these characteristics in the doctoral students' object-related and subject-related contradictions.

First, the object-related primary contradiction was reflected in the object-rules-related and the object-roles-related secondary contradictions; and the subject-related primary contradiction was manifested in the subject-tools-related secondary contradiction. Second, the strategies adopted to resolve the object-related primary contradiction, while ameliorating it to some extent, led to new contradictions (see Chap. 4 for details). Likewise, although the doctoral students' role as expert researchers would gradually prevail as opposed to their role as student researchers, the duality of their roles would, not surprisingly, persist throughout and perhaps beyond their doctoral studies. Third, as discussed in Chaps. 4 and 5, while the secondary contradictions stemming from both the object-related and the subject-related primary contradictions had to do with structural problems and could not be resolved easily, those arising from the latter provided the doctoral students with learning opportunities. More specifically, the contradictions between the object and the rule as well as the object and the roles of the scholarly publishing activity system led the major stakeholders to adopt product-oriented approaches to scholarly publishing, which undermined the doctoral students' processes and experiences of scholarly publishing. By contrast, the contradiction in the doctoral students' developing but still limited grasp and use of some conceptual tools needed for successful scholarly publishing compelled them to resort to cultural artefacts and social others, which provided them with ample learning opportunities.

A conclusion to be drawn from these findings is that the two primary contradictions are inherent in doctoral education and can both constrain and enable doctoral students' participation in and learning of scholarly publishing. It stands to reason that these inner contradictions may well be shared by doctoral students in other contexts, though their manifestations may vary in different contexts.

6.2 Situated Conceptualisation of Doctoral Publication

This study has found that the doctoral students employed the strategy of starting early, orchestrated their own publishing and research activities with those of others, and resorted to various mediating resources in their scholarly publishing activities. These practices were necessitated by the university's publication requirements, the major stakeholders' motives for scholarly publishing, the nature of the nursing discipline, and the rules and norms of scholarly publishing in nursing and neighbouring disciplines. Specifically, in order to address the object-related contradictions, the doctoral students resorted to boundary crossing and/or dynamic reconstruction of the object of the scholarly publishing activity system, which, as shown in Chap. 4, generated new contradictions and undermined the doctoral students' opportunities to participate in and learn scholarly publishing. These findings suggest that scholarly publishing is a dynamically evolving and chronotopically laminated activity.

By contrast, the doctoral students coped with the subject-related contradiction by recourse to various mediating resources, including both cultural artefacts and social others. These mediating resources, as products of human activities themselves, embody the traditions, norms, and conventions of the scholarly publishing activity (Kamler, 2008; Paré, 2010; Starke-Meyerring, 2011). In this sense, these mediating resources also anchor or place the scholarly publishing activity in a specific social, cultural, and historical context. Therefore, scholarly publishing is also a culturally mediated and socially distributed activity (Lundell & Beach, 2003; Prior & Shipka, 2003; Simpson, 2013). Taken together, the findings of this study have shown that scholarly publishing during doctoral candidature is a chronotopically laminated, dynamically evolving, culturally mediated, and socially distributed activity.

In addition, the strategies adopted by the doctoral students to deal with the object-related and subject-related contradictions demonstrate practices of both boundary crossing and LPP. Specifically, the strategies used by the doctoral students to cope with the challenges regarding time pressure exemplify practices of boundary crossing. To alleviate the time pressure, the doctoral students made connections or crossed the boundaries between the scholarly publishing activity system and other activity systems, such as the master's study activity system (Xiao) and the professional work activity system (Fang). By contrast, the strategies employed to handle the challenges stemming from the dual roles of the doctoral students illustrate practices of LPP, i.e., participating in scholarly publishing with the assistance and mediation of social others and cultural artefacts (Lave & Wenger, 1991; Wenger, 1998). In particular, the doctoral students participated in scholarly publishing with the mediation and assistance of cultural artefacts and social others. Notably, the significant roles of journal editors and reviewers also evince that scholarly publishing can afford learning opportunities (Mizzi, 2014; Paré, 2010) and that scholarly socialisation extends beyond the university settings (Casanave, 2010; Lundell & Beach, 2003; Mizzi, 2014). These findings suggest that LPP, a concept employed frequently in previous research to capture the trajectory from novices to experts (see Chap. 2 for a critique of it), alone falls short of giving a comprehensive account of scholarly publishing during doctoral candidature, which involves not only LPP but also boundary crossing.

Moreover, the particular challenges faced and reported by the doctoral students in the present study provide evidence in support of Kwan's (2010, 2013) conceptualisation of scholarly publishing competence as consisting of abilities to draft manuscripts, handle reviews, conceptualise and design publishable research, plan and manage research output, and align thesis and publication (see also Watson, 2012). While the first two types of abilities have been widely documented in the literature, the last three have received relatively little attention in the literature on scholarly publishing (Kwan, 2010, 2013). The challenges stemming from the duality of the object of the scholarly publishing activity system discussed in Chap. 4 indicate that in order to meet the university's publication requirements, doctoral students need to plan and manage their research output (e.g., by bringing along data or research projects from their master's study or professional work), and align the coursework, professional work, and/or thesis activity systems with the scholarly publishing activity system. Likewise, the challenges arising from the dual roles of the subject explicated in Chap. 5 reveal that doctoral students need assistance with their developing repertoires of competence in drafting manuscripts, handling reviews, and conceptualising and designing research to publish their manuscripts successfully. These findings suggest that scholarly publishing during doctoral candidature involves a wide repertoire of knowledge and skills.

Furthermore, the participants in this study took a predominantly critical pragmatic approach to scholarly publishing (see Flowerdew, 2007; Kubota, 2003; Tang, 2012; see also Sect. 2.1), though there were also substantial differences among them, as most evident in their stances on and adoption of the orchestrating strategy. To begin with, all of the participants acknowledged the usefulness and effectiveness of the orchestrating strategy in facilitating scholarly publishing. Despite their recognition of the value of the orchestrating strategy, however, four of the six doctoral students (i.e., Cui, Dong, Fang, and Liang) expressed concerns about its potential ethical ramifications and/or its hindrance to learning. Their stances on the orchestrating strategy in particular and on scholarly publishing in general are characteristic of critical pragmatism (see Benesch, 2001; Hanauer & Englander, 2013; Harwood & Hadley, 2004). The participants' overall critical pragmatic approaches seem to have worked well in that Fang, Wei, and Xiao all graduated on time with the degree, and both Cui and Wu met the graduation requirements in the end, albeit with a one-year and a half-year extension of their candidature, respectively.

Notably, however, Liang refrained from adopting the orchestrating strategy to fulfil the university's publication requirements and had not secured an SCI journal article by the end of her fourth year into the doctoral programme. Although she faced difficulty in timely culling a publication from her longitudinal qualitative thesis project and had some data collected by her seniors at her disposal, she was bent on publishing her own (thesis) research and yearned to publish in Chinese. Her critical approach to the orchestrating strategy, as discussed above and in Chap. 4, might have to do with an ethical dilemma associated with it. Additionally, it may also be related to her "sense-forming motive"—motive not only inducing activity but "also giv[ing] it personal sense" (Leont'ev, 1978/2009, p. 169)—to make her research useful to the disaster survivors and to contribute to the local community, i.e., the process-oriented or experience-oriented object of the scholarly publishing activity system. This commitment to the local community as opposed to the pressure to publish internationally has also been reported by other EAL researchers in previous research (e.g., Duszak & Lewkowicz, 2008; Li & Flowerdew, 2009; Lillis & Curry, 2010; Salager-Meyer, 2008).

Similarly, Fang also had a sense-forming motive to publish her own thesis research rather than others' research to complete the (whole) rite of passage, which she cited as her rationale for her ensuing disapproval of the orchestrating strategy. However, in contrast to Liang, who resisted the orchestrating strategy but did not find an effective alternative, Fang resorted to alternative strategies, i.e., translating research from her professional work into publications and interweaving her thesis research with her publications. These strategies meshed well with both her motive-stimulus—motive only stimulating activity (Leont'ev, 1978/2009)—(i.e., the object of getting published and meeting the university's publication requirements) and sense-forming motive (i.e., the object of completing the rite of passage and becoming a credentialed, if not fully-fledged, researcher). These findings suggest that critical pragmatic approaches seem to be overall effective in attaining the product-oriented object of the scholarly publishing activity, and that it might be risky for doctoral students to resist pragmatic approaches without effective alternatives (see Flowerdew, 2007; Kubota, 2003).

6.3 Limitations and Future Research Directions

The findings of this study should be interpreted with caution considering its several methodological limitations. First, given its focus and design, this study zoomed in and out only on the scholarly publishing activity system and the doctoral study

6.3 Limitations and Future Research Directions

activity system, but not on any specific subsystems of the scholarly publishing activity system. One advantage of activity theory as an analytical lens is its ability to zoom in and out on different levels of actions and activities (Rogoff, 1995; Yamagata-Lynch, 2007, 2010). A multi-dimensional approach (Flowerdew, 2005; Flowerdew & Li, 2009b) or, in this case, a multi-level approach might have provided a fuller and deeper understanding of the doctoral students' scholarly publishing activity. Future research adopting activity theory as its theoretical framework may take a multi-level approach to yield a richer and more comprehensive account of doctoral publication.

Second, another limitation of the present study was its less-than-desirable use of the text-based interviews. Because of its focus on the practices of scholarly publishing, the study did not pay much attention to textual issues that emerged from this study. For instance, had it paid more attention to the texts, it might have generated a more in-depth understanding of the textual strategy of borrowing both Chinese and English source texts in drafting English manuscripts. As noted in Chap. 5, this integrated strategy has received little attention and merits further research. Future research may make better use of text-based interviews and focus more on specific actions involved in manuscript drafting.

Third, for logistic and ethical concerns, this study did not attempt to explore the roles of journal editors and reviewers in the doctoral students' learning of scholarly publishing. The findings of this study showed that journal editors and reviewers were perceived to play a pivotal role in the doctoral students' scholarly publishing activities. It might have shed more light on their roles had the perspectives of journal editors and reviewers been taken into account. However, it was deemed impractical and too intrusive to contact the journal editors and reviewers. In addition, it would also be risky for the doctoral students, considering the high stakes of their publishing efforts. Similarly, the study might also have generated more informative findings about the supervisors' roles had it managed to involve the other supervisor in this study and done more interviews with Professor Liu. Future research may capitalise on the multi-voicedness of activity theory and tap into the perspectives of other stakeholders in doctoral students' scholarly publishing activities.

Fourth, although this study touched upon the influence of disciplinary culture on doctoral students' scholarly publishing practices, it did not delve deeply into it because of its focus and design. Future research may focus on the role of disciplinary culture in doctoral students' scholarly publishing during candidature. A contrastive approach involving two or more different disciplines might prove fruitful for this strand of research. Finally, this study indicated that policies aimed at encouraging doctoral students to publish and enhancing the quality of doctoral education may well have unintended repercussions. The present study constitutes only the first step toward unravelling such repercussions. Policies on doctoral publication obviously warrant more research (Curry & Lillis, 2013).

6.4 Implications for Theory, Policy, and Pedagogy

Drawing on neoliberalism and activity theory and focusing on scholarly publishing within the context of doctoral study, this study has yielded some insights that hold implications for theory, policy, and pedagogy concerning scholarly publishing during doctoral candidature, which are discussed below.

Implications for Theory

Unlike previous research that has centred primarily on the influences of broad geolinguistic and geopolitical contexts on EAL researchers' scholarly publishing practices and/or drawn mostly on situated learning theories to explore the actions or *hows* of scholarly publishing, the present study reveals the influences of the local social and institutional settings on doctoral students' scholarly publishing practices and brings to light not only *how* the doctoral students published their manuscripts during their candidature but also *why* they adopted the strategies and took the actions they did. Drawing on activity systems analyses, this study demonstrates that the participants' dynamically constructed motives for scholarly publishing intersected with the activity settings to bear on the strategies they adopted and the actions they took, such as the doctoral students' adoption of the strategy of orchestrating their own research and publishing activities with those of others. Further, the object—i.e., "the long-term '*why*?'" (Engeström, 1995, p. 411; see also Nardi, 2005) or the "ultimate reason" (Kaptelinin, 2005, p. 5)—for the doctoral students' scholarly publishing activity system is to reproduce knowledge contributors (i.e., develop doctoral students into fully-fledged researchers) and produce knowledge (i.e., make a novel contribution to knowledge). This collective motive or object of the scholarly publishing activity accounts for why the whole doctoral education community of practice engages in scholarly publishing.

This study also contributes to an ongoing effort to theorise scholarly publishing during doctoral candidature by corroborating Kwan's (2013) five-component scholarly publishing competence and by revealing scholarly publishing during doctoral candidature as consisting of both boundary crossing and LPP (Aitchison et al., 2010a; Kamler & Thomson, 2006, 2008; Lee & Kamler, 2008). The findings of this study show that drafting manuscripts, handling manuscripts, and LPP—practices widely documented in the literature—seem to be inadequate to provide a comprehensive portrait of scholarly publishing during doctoral candidature. Other strategies and practices, such as conceptualising and designing publishable research, planning and managing research output, aligning scholarly publishing with other activities, as well as boundary crossing are also integral components of scholarly publishing competence. Moreover, although the expanded conception of scholarly publishing during doctoral candidature is based on a case study in a specific context, it may have theoretical generalisability because the challenges and the coping strategies, from which the expanded conception is derived, stem from primary contradictions in the activity systems of scholarly publishing and doctoral study and are thus inherent in doctoral education.

6.4 Implications for Theory, Policy, and Pedagogy

Implications for Policy

This study reveals that the institutional policies intended to motivate doctoral students to publish during candidature were characteristic of a stick-and-carrot approach with the publication requirements functioning as the stick and the reward schemes serving as the carrot. Relatively little research has examined institutional policies on scholarly publishing, and we still know little about them and their consequences for researchers, especially for doctoral students (Curry & Lillis, 2013). This study constitutes an effort to fill this lacuna.

The university's publication requirements were geared towards ensuring and enhancing the quality of the doctoral programme. Both the professor and the doctoral students endorsed the quality assurance rationale. However, while it served well the purpose of boosting the doctoral students' publication output, it seemed to have not fully achieved its intended goal of ensuring and enhancing the quality of the doctoral programme in that the enormous pressure the university's publication requirements placed on the doctoral students and their supervisors appeared to have transformed their scholarly publishing practices and truncated their learning opportunities and experiences.

Likewise, the various reward schemes instituted by the university to induce the doctoral students to be productive might also lead to problems in the long run, although the participants in the present study did not seem to be particularly interested in them and were concerned mostly about graduation, learning, career preparation, and making knowledge contributions. Those reward schemes, mostly in monetary terms, may exacerbate the already prevailing product-oriented approach to scholarly publishing and doctoral study and "distor[t] the space in which doctoral work is done and research careers are forged" (Aitchison et al., 2010a, p. 2).

Therefore, the findings of this study call for a critical review of publication policies that are intended to encourage doctoral students to publish during candidature and to enhance the quality of doctoral education, but may actually bring about unintended ramifications.

Implications for Pedagogy

In addition to implications for theory and policy, the findings of this study also point to a number of important pedagogical implications. First, the findings of this study demonstrate that the institutional context, the activity settings, and the interdisciplinary nature of the nursing discipline all had a bearing on the doctoral students' scholarly publishing practices. This highlights the importance of "specificity" in scholarly publishing and suggests a need to tailor support for scholarly publishing to institutional and disciplinary contexts and cultures (Hanauer & Englander, 2013; Hyland, 2002).

Second, the present study has shown that the doctoral students' prior experiences with scholarly publishing, their motives for scholarly publishing, as well as their aspirations all played an important role in their scholarly publishing practices. For this reason, it is advisable for universities and supervisors to develop an understanding of their students' prior experiences, motives, and aspirations (Flowerdew & Habibie,

2022; Phillips, 2016). For example, in this study, it would be of great help to understand Fang's longing to complete the rite of the passage of doctoral study, Liang's craving to publish her own thesis research and contribute to the local community, and Xiao's experience of working on an English manuscript during her master's study. Such knowledge can be utilised to facilitate their scholarly publishing endeavours and doctoral studies. Take Liang's case for example. Her supervisor could have paid more attention to her desire to publish her own thesis research and to contribute to the local community while working with her to plan her research and publishing output and align her publication with her thesis research, which might have prevented her protracted delay in meeting the university's publication requirements.

Third, the findings of this study reveal the complexity and often occludedness of scholarly publishing (e.g., professors' rationales for selecting research topics, the norms and expectations of handling reviews). This underscores the need for explicit instruction and articulation on various aspects of scholarly publishing (Cargill et al., 2012; Hanauer & Englander, 2013; Li & Flowerdew, 2020). Hanauer and Englander (2013), for example, recommend that "courses, workshops, and presentations incorporate this explicit instruction" (p. 139). As pointed out earlier in this study, sharing sessions given by published students and talks or seminars conducted by journal editors can demystify some of the tacit issues involved in scholarly publishing and help doctoral students better navigate the complex and occluded process.

Moreover, this study corroborates the expanded conception of scholarly publishing proposed by Kwan (2010, 2013), which posits that scholarly publishing competence consists of not only abilities to write up manuscripts and handle reviews but also abilities to conceptualise and design publishable research projects, plan and manage research output, and align scholarly publishing activities with other activities. While the first two types of ability involve language expertise, the other three require content expertise. This underlines the importance of covering both discursive and non-discursive domains in intervention and support for scholarly publishing (Hanauer & Englander, 2013; Kwan, 2010, 2013). Seminars, workshops, or talks conducted by supervisors or other content experts can be useful for doctoral students to obtain an overview of the non-discursive domains of scholarly publishing.

More importantly, the expanded conception of scholarly publishing competence also points to the need for content specialists and language professionals to collaborate with each other to facilitate doctoral students' scholarly publishing endeavours (Cargill et al., 2012; Flowerdew, 2015; Hanauer & Englander, 2013; Kwan, 2010, 2013). One area that can benefit greatly from such collaboration is fostering doctoral students' attempts to align their publications with their thesis projects, which requires both discursive strategies and content expertise.

Fourth, the findings of this study show that it is not enough for universities to offer sporadic and one-off seminars, workshops, or talks on scholarly publishing. As the doctoral students pointed out, this form of instruction might be well equipped to help them learn about some general rules of scholarly publishing, but they proved inadequate to help them develop an in-depth knowledge of the rules, norms, and practices of scholarly publishing and provide them with little hands-on experience with writing. Therefore, to complement such support, there is a need to offer formal courses on scholarly publishing, especially on its discursive domains (e.g., writing up manuscripts) (Hanauer & Englander, 2013). Further, this study also demonstrates that the doctoral students differed substantially from each other in their publishing practices and strategies. This suggests the need to provide different types of support and intervention to meet doctoral students' divergent needs (Hanauer & Englander, 2013). Therefore, in addition to seminars, talks, workshops, and formal courses, editorial services and writing centres also have a role to play in offering tailored support to doctoral students whenever they run into difficulties in drafting their manuscripts (Hanauer & Englander, 2013; Li & Flowerdew, 2007).

Finally, this study reveals that while universities and supervisors tend to provide product-oriented support, doctoral students need ongoing process-oriented support. This points to the need for better communication between university administrators and supervisors on the one hand, and doctoral students on the other, about their expectations for each other. Meanwhile, the different expectations are reflective of a dilemma faced by the major stakeholders. On the one hand, they may feel pressured to ensure on-time graduation with the degree, as evident in the present study, which seems to require a product-oriented or pragmatic approach. On the other hand, despite their overriding concern about the product and outcome of scholarly publishing, they may also be invested in the process and experience of scholarly publishing and doctoral study, as evidenced in this study by the doctoral students' and supervisors' interest in learning, career preparation, and knowledge contribution.

Notably, as discussed in Chap. 4, the product- and process-oriented approaches are not dichotomous but dialectical. In other words, the major stakeholders are not faced with an either-or dilemma. Therefore, what is needed is perhaps a more balanced approach, which, while focusing on attaining the product and outcome, also pays attention to doctoral students' process and experience of scholarly publishing and doctoral study. This calls for genuine interest and continuous investment in doctoral students' attempts at scholarly publishing and at becoming fully-fledged researchers. Regular meetings with supervisors as well as editorial services and writing centres may provide doctoral students with the much-needed ongoing process-oriented support. Such ongoing process-oriented support can not only facilitate doctoral students' scholarly publishing output but also make scholarly publishing during doctoral candidature a more positive and enriching experience.

References

Aitchison, C., Kamler, B., & Lee, A. (2010). Introduction: Why publishing pedagogies? In C. Aitchison, B. Kamler, & A. Lee (Eds.), *Publishing pedagogies for the doctorate and beyond* (pp. 1–11). Routledge.

Aitchison, C., Catterall, J., Ross, P., & Burgin, S. (2012). 'Tough love and tears': Learning doctoral writing in the sciences. *Higher Education Research & Development, 31*, 435–447. https://doi.org/10.1080/07294360.2011.559195

Beauchamp, C., Jazvac-Martek, M., & McAlpine, L. (2009). Studying doctoral education: Using activity theory to shape methodological tools. *Innovations in Education and Teaching International, 46*, 265–277. https://doi.org/10.1080/14703290903068839

Benesch, S. (2001). *Critical English for academic purposes: Theory, politics, pratice.* Lawrence Erlbaum.

Bonneau, C. (2013, July 4–6). Contradictions and their concrete manifestations: An activity-theoretical analysis of the intra-organizational co-configuration of open source software. In *The 29th EGOS Colloquium*, Montréal, Canada.

Boud, D., & Lee, A. (2009). Introduction. In D. Boud & A. Lee (Eds.), *Changing practices of doctoral education* (pp. 1–9). Routledge.

Cargill, M., O'Connor, P., & Li, Y. (2012). Educating Chinese scientists to write for international journals: Addressing the divide between science and technology education and English language teaching. *English for Specific Purposes, 31*, 60–69. https://doi.org/10.1016/j.esp.2011.05.003

Casanave, C. P. (2010). Dovetailing under impossible circumstances. In C. Aitchison, B. Kamler, & A. Lee (Eds.), *Publishing pedagogies for the doctorate and beyond* (pp. 47–63). Routledge.

Cole, M., & Engeström, Y. (1993). A cultural-historical approach to distributed cognition. In G. Salomon (Ed.), *Distributed cognitions: Psychological and educational considerations* (pp. 1–46). Cambridge University Press.

Collinson, J. A. (2006). Just 'non-academics'?: Research administrators and contested occupational identity. *Work, Employment & Society, 20*, 267–288. https://doi.org/10.1177/0950017006064114

Curry, M. J., & Lillis, T. (2013). Introduction to the thematic issue: Participating in academic publishing—consequences of linguistic policies and practices. *Language Policy, 12*, 209–213. https://doi.org/10.1007/s10993-013-9286-7

Delamont, S., Parry, O., Atkinson, P., & Hiken, A. (1994). Suspended between two stools: Doctoral students in British higher education. In A. Coffey & P. Atkinson (Eds.), *Occupational socialization and working lives* (pp. 138–53). Avebury.

Delamont, S., Atkinson, P., & Parry, O. (2000). *The doctoral experience: Success and failure in graduate school.* Falmer Press.

Duszak, A., & Lewkowicz, J. (2008). Publishing academic texts in English: A Polish perspective. *Journal of English for Academic Purposes, 7*, 108–120. https://doi.org/10.1016/j.jeap.2008.03.001

Engeström, Y. (1987). *Learning by expanding: An activity-theoretical approach to developmental research.* Orienta-Konsultit.

Engeström, Y. (1995). Objects, contradictions and collaboration in medical cognition: An activity-theoretical perspective. *Artificial Intelligence in Medicine, 7*, 395–412. https://doi.org/10.1016/0933-3657(95)00012-U

Engeström, Y. (1999). Activity theory and individual and social transformation. In Y. Engeström, R. Miettinen, & R. Punamäki (Eds.), *Perspectives on activity theory* (pp. 19–38). Cambridge University Press.

Engeström, Y. (2000). Activity theory as a framework for analyzing and redesigning work. *Ergonomics, 43*, 960–974. https://doi.org/10.1080/001401300409143

Engeström, Y. (2001). Expansive learning at work: Toward an activity theoretical reconceptualization. *Journal of Education and Work, 14*, 133–156.

Engeström, Y., Engeström, R., & Kärkkäinen, M. (1995). Polycontextuality and boundary crossing in expert cognition: Learning and problem solving in complex work activities. *Learning and Instruction, 5*, 319–336. https://doi.org/10.1016/0959-4752(95)00021-6

Engeström, Y., & Miettinen, R. (1999). Introduction. In Y. Engeström, R. Miettinen, & R. Punamäki (Eds.), *Perspectives on activity theory* (pp. 1–16). Cambridge University Press.

Flowerdew, J. (2005). A multimodal approach to research into processes of scholarly writing for publications. In P. K. Matsuda & T. Silva (Eds.), *Second language writing research: Perspectives on the process of knowledge construction* (pp. 65–77). Lawrence Erlbaum.

Flowerdew, J. (2007). The non-Anglophone scholar on the periphery of scholarly publication. *AILA Review, 20*, 14–27. https://doi.org/10.1075/aila.20.04flo

Flowerdew, J. (2015). Some thoughts on English for Research Publication Purposes (ERPP) and related issues. *Language Teaching, 48*, 250–262. https://doi.org/10.1017/S0261444812000523

Flowerdew, J., & Habibie, P. (2022). *Introducing English for research publication purposes.* Routledge.

Flowerdew, J., & Li, Y. (2009). The globalisation of scholarship: Studying Chinese scholars writing for international publication. In R. M. Manchón (Ed.), *Writing in foreign language contexts: Learning, teaching, and research* (pp. 156–182). Multilingual Matters.

Foot, K. A. (2014). Cultural-historical activity theory: Exploring a theory to inform practice and research. *Journal of Human Behavior in the Social Environment, 24*, 329–347. https://doi.org/10.1080/10911359.2013.831011

Hanauer, D. I., & Englander, K. (2013). *Scientific writing in a second language.* Parlor Press.

Harwood, N., & Hadley, G. (2004). Demystifying institutional practices: Critical pragmatism and the teaching of academic writing. *English for Specific Purposes, 23*, 355–377. https://doi.org/10.1016/s0889-4906(03)00058-9

Hyland, K. (2002). Specificity revisited: How far should we go now? *English for Specific Purposes, 21*, 385–395. https://doi.org/10.1016/S0889-4906(01)00028-X

Kamler, B. (2008). Rethinking doctoral publication practices: Writing from and beyond the thesis. *Studies in Higher Education, 33*, 283–294. https://doi.org/10.1080/03075070802049236

Kamler, B., & Thomson, P. (2006). *Helping doctoral students write: Pedagogies for supervision.* Routledge.

Kamler, B., & Thomson, P. (2008). The failure of dissertation advice books: Toward alternative pedagogies for doctoral writing. *Educational Researcher, 37*, 507–514. https://doi.org/10.3102/0013189x08327390

Kandiko, C. B., & Kinchin, I. M. (2012). What is a doctorate? A concept-mapped analysis of process versus product in the supervision of lab-based PhDs. *Educational Research, 54*, 3–16. https://doi.org/10.1080/00131881.2012.658196

Kaptelinin, V. (2005). The object of activity: Making sense of the sense-maker. *Mind, Culture, and Activity, 12*, 4–18. https://doi.org/10.1207/s15327884mca1201_2

Kubota, R. (2003). Striving for original voice in publication?: A critical reflection. In C. P. Casanave & S. Vandrick (Eds.), *Writing for scholarly publication: Behind the scenes in language education* (pp. 73–83). Lawrence Erlbaum.

Kuutti, K. (1996). Activity theory as a potential framework for human-computer interaction research. In B. A. Nardi (Ed.), *Context and consciousness: Activity theory and human-computer interaction* (pp. 17–44). MIT Press.

Kwan, B. S. C. (2010). An investigation of instruction in research publishing offered in doctoral programs: The Hong Kong case. *Higher Education, 59*, 55–68. https://doi.org/10.1007/s10734-009-9233-x

Kwan, B. S. C. (2013). Facilitating novice researchers in project publishing during the doctoral years and beyond: A Hong Kong-based study. *Studies in Higher Education, 38*, 207–225. https://doi.org/10.1080/03075079.2011.576755

Lave, J., & Wenger, E. (1991). *Situated learning: Legitimate peripheral participation.* Cambridge University Press.

Lee, A., & Kamler, B. (2008). Bringing pedagogy to doctoral publishing. *Teaching in Higher Education, 13*, 511–523. https://doi.org/10.1080/13562510802334723

Lee, H., & Lee, K. (2013). Publish (in international indexed journals) or perish: Neoliberal ideology in a Korean university. *Language Policy, 12*, 215–230. https://doi.org/10.1007/s10993-012-9267-2

Leont'ev, A. N. (1978/2009). *Activity, consciousness, and personality.* Marxists Internet Archive (Sourced from the edition published in 1978 by Prentice-Hall).

Li, Y., & Flowerdew, J. (2007). Shaping Chinese novice scientists' manuscripts for publication. *Journal of Second Language Writing, 16*, 100–117. https://doi.org/10.1016/j.jslw.2007.05.001

Li, Y., & Flowerdew, J. (2009). International engagement versus local commitment: Hong Kong academics in the humanities and social sciences writing for publication. *Journal of English for Academic Purposes, 8*, 279–293. https://doi.org/10.1016/j.jeap.2009.05.002

Li, Y., & Flowerdew, J. (2020). Teaching English for Research Publication Purposes (ERPP): A review of language teachers' pedagogical initiatives. *English for Specific Purposes, 59*, 29–41. https://doi.org/10.1016/j.esp.2020.03.002

Lillis, T., & Curry, M. J. (2010). *Academic writing in a global context: The politics and practices of publishing in English*. Routledge.

Lundell, D. B., & Beach, R. (2003). Dissertation writers' negotiations with competing activity systems. In C. Bazerman & D. Russell (Eds.), *Writing selves/Writing societies* (pp. 483–514). The WAC Clearinghouse.

McGrail, M. R., Rickard, C. M., & Jones, R. (2006). Publish or perish: A systematic review of interventions to increase academic publication rates. *Higher Education Research & Development, 25*, 19–35. https://doi.org/10.1080/07294360500453053

Mizzi, R. C. (2014). Writing realities: An exploration of drawbacks and benefits of publishing while enrolled in a doctoral program. *New Horizons in Adult Education and Human Resource Development, 26*, 54–59. https://doi.org/10.1002/nha3.20063

Nardi, B. A. (2005). Objects of desire: Power and passion in collaborative activity. *Mind, Culture, and Activity, 12*, 37–51. https://doi.org/10.1207/s15327884mca1201_4

Paré, A. (2010). Slow the presses: Concerns for premature publication. In C. Aitchison, B. Kamler, & A. Lee (Eds.), *Publishing pedagogies for the doctorate and beyond* (pp. 30–46). Routledge.

Parry, S. (2007). *Disciplines and doctorates: Higher education dynamics*. Springer.

Phillips, T. (2016). Writing center support for graduate students: An integrated model. In S. Simpson, N. A. Caplan, M. Cox, & T. Phillips (Eds.), *Supporting graduate student writers: Research, curriculum, and program design* (pp. 159–170). University of Michigan Press.

Prior, P. (1994). Response, revision, disciplinarity. *Written Communication, 11*, 483–533. https://doi.org/10.1177/0741088394011004003

Prior, P. (1997). Literate activity and disciplinarity: The heterogeneous (re)production of American Studies around a graduate seminar. *Mind, Culture, and Activity, 4*, 275–295. https://doi.org/10.1207/s15327884mca0404_5

Prior, P. (1998). *Writing/disciplinarity: A sociohistoric account of literate activity in the academy*. Lawrence Erlbaum.

Prior, P., & Min, Y. K. (2008). The lived experience of graduate work and writing: From chronotopic laminations to everyday lamentations. In C. P. Casanave & X. Li (Eds.), *Learning the literate practices of graduate school: Insiders' reflections on academic enculturation* (pp. 230–246). University of Michigan Press.

Prior, P., & Shipka, J. (2003). Chronotropic lamination: Tracing the contours of literate activity. In C. Bazerman & D. R. Russell (Eds.), *Writing selves/Writing societies: Research from activity perspectives* (pp. 180–238). The WAC Clearinghous.

Rogoff, B. (1995). Observing sociocultural activity on three planes: Participatory appropriation, guided participation, and apprenticeship. In J. V. Wertsch, P. del Rio, & A. Alvarez (Eds.), *Sociocultural studies of mind* (pp. 139–164). Cambridge University Press.

Roth, W.-M., & Lee, Y.-J. (2007). "Vygotsky's neglected legacy": Cultural-historical activity theory. *Review of Educational Research, 77*, 186–232. https://doi.org/10.3102/0034654306298273

Russell, D. R. (1997). Rethinking genre in school and society: An activity theory analysis. *Written Communication, 14*, 504–554. https://doi.org/10.1177/0741088397014004004

Salager-Meyer, F. (2008). Scientific publishing in developing countries: Challenges for the future. *Journal of English for Academic Purposes, 7*, 121–132. https://doi.org/10.1016/j.jeap.2008.03.009

Simpson, S. (2013). Systems of writing response: A Brazilian student's experiences writing for publication in an environmental sciences doctoral program. *Research in the Teaching of English, 48*, 228–249.

Sinclair, J., Barnacle, R., & Cuthbert, D. (2014). How the doctorate contributes to the formation of active researchers: What the research tells us. *Studies in Higher Education, 39*, 1972–1986. https://doi.org/10.1080/03075079.2013.806460

Starfield, S. (2004). 'Why does this feel empowering?': Thesis writing, concordancing, and the corporatizing university. In B. Norton & K. Toohey (Eds.), *Critical pedagogies and language learning* (pp. 138–157). Cambridge University Press.

Starke-Meyerring, D. (2011). The paradox of writing in doctoral education: Student experiences. In L. McAlpine & C. Amundsen (Eds.), *Doctoral education: Research-based strategies for doctoral students, supervisors and administrators* (pp. 75–95). Springer.

Tang, R. (2012). The issues and challenges facing academic writers from ESL/EFL contexts: An overview. In R. Tang (Ed.), *Academic writing in a second or foreign language: Issues and challenges facing ESL/EFL academic writers in higher education contexts* (pp. 1–18). Continuum.

Watson, M. (Ed.). (2012). *Publication practices and multilingual professionals in US universities: Towards critical perspectives on administration and pedagogy*. The WAC Clearinghouse.

Wenger, E. (1998). *Communities of practice: Learning, meaning, and identity*. Cambridge University Press.

Yamagata-Lynch, L. C. (2007). Confronting analytical dilemmas for understanding complex human interactions in design-based research from a cultural-historical activity theory (CHAT) framework. *Journal of the Learning Sciences, 16*, 451–484. https://doi.org/10.1080/10508400701524777

Yamagata-Lynch, L. C. (2010). *Activity systems analysis methods: Understanding complex learning environments*. Springer.

Printed in the United States
by Baker & Taylor Publisher Services